BE...

D1616966

MARNY JAASTAD

LIVE YOUR DREAM PUBLISHING

SOLANA BEACH, CA 92075

Be...

Live Your Dream Publishing

Solana Beach, CA

marnymarie@yahoo.com

ISBN: 1530883997

ISBN 13: 978-1530883998

This book is dedicated to………..EVAN!

Preface

It was Christmas 2012. My godson, Evan, was 11 and wise beyond his years. I of course had always thought he was brilliant. I believe this was the first year that he actually chose my gifts himself. I received a pair of earrings with little hearts and cats on them and an item that would BE-come this book.

Who could have thought that a small, silver stand with the small, simple word BE followed by three ellipses would have such an immense impact upon my life. Along with the stand came a burlap bag with 72 rectangular, green cards inside. Upon each card was printed a word or a phrase that one could slide into the three ellipses, therefore reading "BE excited", for example. As I opened the gift, I recall thinking, "Oh what a perfectly unique, MARNY sort of gift." How were either of us to know the monster that had been unleashed! A good and kind monster, mind you, but a growing and hungry one at the same time.

Initially the idea was but a mere nugget in my brain. However as it percolated back there, it swelled and grew and took on true edges and definition until.....VOILA! What you hold in your hands had come to life. I decided that I would select one word every week and place it in the stand – which I also placed above my desk so that it would catch my eye on a regular basis. (And yes, sometimes, as you will see, a week became three). I would ponder (and pontificate) on what that word or phrase meant to me. Or meant in the scope of the world. Or merely in the context of my relationship with Evan.

And so began my literary journey as the exploration of how to BE a person, a being on this planet, among others, as a unique individual. And as appropriate as any ironic situation could be, my first pick, on Christmas Day of course was to BE...GIVING! Yes, really. And so it began. Two and half years of selecting and thinking and writing about simple words or phrases connected to me and to Evan by the word BE. Though it has been mostly a one-way conversation, it has been the most fulfilling, eye-opening, and deeply personal exercise I have ever undertaken. As Evan grew and matured over the three years, my aim was to provide my part of "the village" that it takes to raise a child.

From a simple, silver stand and the simple word BE has arisen what I hope will be as insightful and exploratory for you and your loved ones as it was for me.

A Note about the Presentation and Author

The entries in this book are presented as they were written in emails at that time. I have left them un-doctored save for a few grammatical and spelling errors which might have altered the intent of the entry. Each entry is the equivalent of a brain-Polaroid at that point in both my and Evan's lives. The series follows the evolution of our relationship as well as each of us independently.

I've tried to add no additional thoughts or details as hindsight can often skew the purity of "The Now." Where it seemed appropriate and necessary, I have added brief background information so that the reader may have a better point of reference for the entry. To clear any confusion over references to mothers in the book, "Mom" when it appears is Evan's mom. If I am referring to MY mom, the writing will indicate "my mom."

The choice of lapis for the background on the cover of the book draws from the ancient Egyptian belief that the lapis stone represented TRUTH!

My various professions have changed dramatically over the years. However, my curiosity and fascination with how we become who we are has been a constant. I started with an MBA in Health Care, working in the community health center system in Boston. From there I became a member of the US National Rowing Team, competing nationally and internationally for several years. My last station in life – for the past 15 years – has been as a personal trainer in a gym in Southern California for the past 13 years and in Georgia prior to that for two years.

I have always been a student of the human mind and its power. My major at Tufts University was Bio-Psychology. Motivation and drive, our carrots and sticks, are as diverse as we all are. I have taken care of and watched over people from the time of being a resident assistant in college to coaching collegiate athletes to personal training people - which for many is a cheaper version of therapy! How each of these people became who they are is always fascinating to me. When Evan's gift arrived that Christmas, it could not have been more perfect.

The Chapters

GIVING

(POSITIVE, CONFIDENT, ON TOP OF YOUR GAME)

From: **Marny Jaastad** (marnymarie@yahoo.com)

To: evanmccleerybrown@yahoo.com

Date: Thursday, January 3, 2013 2:42PM

Hi Evan

I absolutely LOVE my "Be...." gift. And mostly I love it because every time I pick a new word, I think about you first - because you gave me the gift - and then I move onto think about how I might BE whatever the word or phrase is.

When I first opened the present, I thought I would change the word every day but it has seemed that I need some of them to linger a bit longer - to think about them a bit more or to achieve the stated "goal."

So today as I was thinking about the word that was currently in the stand - THOUGHTFUL - I _thought_.....HEY, I'll write to Evan every time I pick a new word and tell him what the word is and how I have tried to do or BE that action or phrase....

You can comment on them or not, or read them - OR NOT! haha But I hope you don't mind that I will write to you with each of these. And who knows how much I will learn about myself and others over time as I work my way through all of the cards in the little bag.

I have a little catching up to do. It'll be quick, don't worry!

Xmas Day - Be GIVING! How appropriate! And I picked it randomly, eyes closed!   Well that was easy to achieve on Xmas Day.

Next was Be POSITIVE. I had a few people who were frustrating me at work so I tried very hard to see all of the good things that I like about being at work and the people I work with; even if a few of them might have made me sad.

Then Be CONFIDENT. That was a good one for me to get. Sometimes I question myself about decisions that I am trying to make. I have learned that my first instinct is usually my best and so I really try to go with that. I also still had this one up on a day I went to a really hard yoga class and I decided that instead of being concerned that I might not be able to do a certain movement, I was confident that I could - and I DID! yay!

Last was Be ON TOP OF YOUR GAME. It reminded me every day that I go to work to give people the best of me. And that my clients deserve to have my very best. If I am not on top of my game, I need to ask myself why - tired?

overworked? distracted? And then fix those problems and get back on it!

And here we are at the current one....Be THOUGHTFUL.
And for now, my thoughtfulness is that I think of you and your family and how much you all mean to me and how I can try to show you all how important you are in my life.

And I have also tried to be a little less rushed and pressured in my day so that I can let others go through a door before me or take the last towel at work or even just smile when someone is obviously not having a good day.

Thanks for listening! It helps me to reflect on my day and my actions. Something everyone should do every once in a while!

Love you,
Marny

THOUGHTFUL

I actually still have this word up as it seems to be a very good guiding principle in life in general......so today as I was thinking about being thoughtful, I decided that I would be thoughtful TO ME! And by that I mean talking nicely to myself even when I feel like I didn't do what I wanted to do. I realized that some days we just don't feel as good as we do other days and we have to be as nice to ourselves as we would be to someone else having a "bad" day.

So I hope YOU are having a great day. Sorry school starts back tomorrow....yuk, never fun to come off of vacation. But at least you will get to see all of your friends again!
love, Marny

INVENTIVE

Subject: BE...INVENTIVE!

From: **Marny Jaastad** (marnymarie@yahoo.com)

To: evanmccleerybrown@yahoo.com

Date: Sunday, January 13, 2013 2:09PM

Oh boy. So I finally moved on from being THOUGHTFUL. I'm not giving up on it, but I felt like I wanted a new challenge. And did I ever pick a good one - INVENTIVE. I am still pondering how I am going to be inventive - beyond the crazy things that I rig up at work for people to do exercises with.
Beyond the Einstein and MacGyver kinds of stuff I am not sure how else one practices being inventive but maybe I'll invent other ways - haha.
I'll let you know what I come up with. And I also wonder whether inventive is different from creative, or maybe just a subset of it......

Oh and sorry about Notre Dame - BUMMMMMER, huh??? Jeeez they looked so stunned that first half. Oh well, as it is said, there is always NEXT year......
Love, Marny

Have you got any good inventions going on????

From: **Marny Jaastad** (marnymarie@yahoo.com)

To: evanmccleerybrown@yahoo.com

Date: Sunday, January 19, 2013 6:08AM

Ok so I wasn't the most INVENTIVE person ever this week. It's funny though because I found myself thinking about being inventive....looking for opportunities to do something differently or work around something that was broken in the gym.

I did have to rig up a couple of contraptions for one of my clients who is currently suffering with a lot of general body pain and cannot manage certain positions. So I sort of had to "build" her some things that would mimic machines that I might have used instead. Interesting to think about.
Maybe I will REALLY invent something someday and revolutionize exercising all over the world! HAHA Well, one can always dream. Until then I will continue to look for new and better ways to do things. Who knows what might come of it!

Now for my new word.......I just picked: KIND-HEARTED.
Ohhhh this is a GOOD one for me. I know that I can sometimes be a little intolerant with people when they are moving slower than I want them to. Or if I am at a store and the clerk is really slow......And mostly I know I can be pretty tough on myself. Maybe that will be my first goal.....be kind-hearted to myself which will then allow me to do the same with others.
xoxo
Marny

How's the Foosball table?!??!

KIND-
HEARTED

From: **Marny Jaastad** (marnymarie@yahoo.com)

To: evanmccleerybrown@yahoo.com

Date: Sunday, January 27, 2013 2:32 PM

BE...ing kind-hearted has been interesting for me - because I like to think that in general I AM kind-hearted to people. I love being nice to people but what I thought about and noticed over this past week is that being kind-hearted ain't just about bein' NICE!

So you know when someone makes you mad because they do something that kind of messes up what you were planning to do or what you wanted to do during the day? What I found myself doing this week, because this happens ALLLLL the time with my clients, is that I would say very loudly - in my head of course so no one thought I was crazy - KIND-HEARTED!!! It wasn't a matter of being nice at all, it was simply realizing that they are not INTENDING to "mess up my day." And in reality they haven't messed up anything. Being kind-hearted made me relax a bit and not get as wound up and uptight when my "rules" weren't being followed.

I was also more kind to myself. I tried to be patient with myself when I was doing things that I might have expected more from myself. And ya know what??? Sometimes when you relax and don't put a lot of pressure on yourself to do great things.....great things happen anyway!

Onto the next Be.......BACKED-UP

hmmmmmm this is gonna be a toughie.....I am not even sure what that means! (other than my computer! hahahah)
THOUGHTS from you!?!?!??!
Love, Marny

BACKED-UP

Be...BACKED-UP

From: **Marny Jaastad** (marnymarie@yahoo.com)

To: evanmccleerybrown@yahoo.com

Date: Wednesday, February 6, 2013 3:46 AM

Hey Ev!

All right, what started out as what I thought would be VERY tough for me to have something to write about or even to think about became very apparent in meaning for me.....

What a week it has been with things that made (me) realize being backed up isn't just about my computer!
What I came to realize is that being backed up is many things.

1. Have a Plan B. It has taken me a long time to learn that my best laid plans - and boy am I am planner! - are not always going to go the way I want them to, and maybe not anywhere near where I want them to go. So there is always some sort of other path in the back of my head that I can take. For instance at work this week, my boss resigned. He is a great guy and things will change a lot when he leaves. So I am starting to think about what else I might do or where else I might go since it may not be the best place to work once changes occur. But I had already been looking at different options that I might have and talking with anyone who offered other ideas and jobs that I could do. So we'll see but I know that I will be ok because I was backed up! haha

2. You never know when you might need someone to help you out. Sometimes they come out of nowhere and give you something you didn't even know you needed. Basically I have found that trying to be good and do good in the world actually does pay off! The place that I do yoga is really great so I have been referring people to join and many of them have. And they have been as happy there as I am. Well, last week the managers at the yoga studio called me into the office - OH NO! How can I be in trouble I thought, I don't even work here! But they told me they were so grateful to me for promoting them and sending them clients that they gave me a 3 month unlimited membership - FREE!!! I was so so so surprised and happy. What a great thing. It is very expensive so I am careful about how much I go because I pay for each class, but

this means I can go whenever I want - sometimes twice a day! - and it won't cost me anything. So keeping connections to people and places that you go a lot helps to make (sure) they "have your back" as the saying goes.

3. Always have in your life at least one person who you can call, write, text, Skype, or by whatever means at any time of (the) day or night and they will always support you no matter what. Your mom is my backup. She always listens to me, always supports me, always has my best interest at heart (even when I don't always like what she says, haha).

So I am pretty excited about what I have learned about myself and about the importance of being BACKED UP. I think no matter what age you are, it is an important part of life.

I will always have your back, Evan. And your family and friends will always support and back whatever it is you are doing or want to do.

Love, Marny
Oh - and my next word is..............BE...FULL OF GRACE.
Ohhhh I am going to love this one!

FULL OF
GRACE

From: **Marny Jaastad** (marnymarie@yahoo.com)

To: evanmccleerybrown@yahoo.com

Date: Wednesday, February 13, 2013 7:53 AM

Hey Ev!

Sometimes with these little phrases and words I feel like someone is reading them over my shoulder and then "setting me up" to fall into situations where I will have to practice them! hahaha Either that or it's like when you get something new like a shirt or sneakers or a car and suddenly you see that same thing everywhere! I am guessing that it's the 2nd one and I don't have some little ghost following me around......at least I hope so!

 So I had a couple of really big ones with "being graceful" about something that happened to me, or around me.

One day I was in 2 different classes, on Sunday the first was Pure Barre and a lady came in late - not 5 minutes late but like 20! And they let her in. At first I was really mad because it totally disrupts class and then she's not up to speed with what's going on. I thought I would call the studio afterwards and complain but then decided not to because I thought to myself...maybe something bad had happened and she just couldn't possibly get to class on time. And maybe this was the only time that she could make it all week and this might have been her one little bit of time for herself.

THEN only a few hours later I was in yoga and it was packed and AGAIN about 15 minutes into class TWO people came in late. And of course, 1 of them comes and plops down right next to me. Now it is REALLY tight and we've all been going along and here he is having to get set up and try to figure out where we are and stretch out and warm up a little, etc......Again I was going to say something to the front desk when I left. I thought to myself, you know, this has happened twice in one day to me for a reason. And so I challenged myself to forget about him and just practice my yoga.......and it worked. It didn't seem all that important anymore. (BUT if he does it again next week, all bets are off! hahaha You only get 1 chance to make the same mistake with me. Well not really, but you know what I mean).

There is also kind of a funny thing that goes on at the gym with the fans and people arguing over whether they want them on or off. I personally do not like them at all but if someone is on a machine and using the fan and it blows on me I don't ask them to turn it off if they were there first. I ask them to do it when they are done, but I don't disturb them or make a fuss. I went to do a workout this week and a woman was arguing with a man about turning off the fan. I know this man and he ALWAYS has the fan on, I don't even bother to ask. She was not very nice to him and so when he left, he did not turn off the fan (she had asked him to) and she got REALLY mad at him and called him names and then made a big deal about turning it off and how it interrupted her workout. When I was younger I would have been the exact same way. I always thought that other people were getting in my way when I was doing something - driving, shopping, working out, whatever. If they impacted what I was trying to do, I got super angry. But I realized that he is not being mean to me by turning on the fan, he is HOT. I just put on another shirt and I am fine with it.

It's funny when you have a little reminder - like BE....full of grace - to help you see situations in a different way......

Thank you again for giving me this present. You may not ever know how much it has helped me learn about myself and how it has helped me try to be a better person.

Love, Marny

I really hope you don't hate these emails!!!!

I'll let you know what I pick next when I get home from work today.

HONEST

Subject:	**Be...Honest!**
From:	**Marny Jaastad** (marnymarie@yahoo.com)
To:	evanmccleerybrown@yahoo.com
Date:	Sunday, February 24, 2013 5:41 PM

Just picked this one over the weekend...
Well this will be both easy and hard. I consider myself to be VERY honest with others. Liars always get caught is my philosophy.

BUT it is easy to not always be honest with yourself.....so this is my challenge to me. I have to ask myself if I am always being honest about what I want to be doing, how I am feeling, etc in my day.....hmmmmm

Hope you HONESTLY have a good day! hahaha

Marny

Oh - you must be off from school for President's Day. Hope you can get outside and have some fun.

Welllll, yet another interesting (one) to get me looking at the world and myself. So I was wrong, mostly, about it being tough to be honest with myself. I actually was quite good at it! Brutally so sometimes! hahaha

It was funny though because I did find myself being a little more blunt with people. If they asked me a question about something that I might usually hedge on answering - "am I not as strong as I was last week?" or "do you think I am making a good decision?" I answered straight away and with my exact opinion. But not in a mean way, in a very HONEST way and then adding why I thought as I did and trying to help them understand that my opinion of something was not my JUDGMENT of them, just my analysis of the situation. What I finally concluded yesterday, after 3 different events arose that all showed me how people were being dishonest, was that in the end honesty begins with YOU (or me, or whomever). I observe that so many people are dishonest in their daily lives and interactions with others because they are initially dishonest with themselves. I still believe that being able to look yourself in the face - whether literally, with a mirror, or figuratively within your own brain - and KNOW that you are being honest and truthful with yourself in your actions is the first and most important step in being honest in all that you do.

It also struck me that being dishonest really just takes a whole lot of time, energy and effort which I'd rather put towards doing some FUN stuff - like flying on a trapeze *(hahaha) Once you are dishonest, or lie, about something you then have to continue so as to not be caught in the lie......too much work. Just be straight.....always.

And now we move onto Be....DILIGENT. Again, I think I am VERY diligent but every new word surprises me with what it opens my eyes up to.....
Lots of love,
Marny

*Evan had visited me the previous fall and we had gone to a flying trapeze class.

DILIGENT

From: **Marny Jaastad** (marnymarie@yahoo.com)

To: evanmccleerybrown@yahoo.com

Date: Monday, March 4, 2013 3:44 AM

Though I consider myself to be VERY diligent, I decided to look this word up in the dictionary to see the various meanings that it might have. Though some of the words I have picked seem to have multiple meanings - and I have interpreted them in less conventional ways, diligent seemed pretty cut and dried.

This is what came up: showing steady and earnest care and effort. Ok, so that's pretty much me in everything that I do! Well, at least I like to think so.
What I discovered is that while I am very diligent at work and in my interactions with others, I am often not as steadfast when I have personal projects that I am working on. So instead of the things that I saw and did and learned this week about "my word" what I am going to do with diligent is more about moving forward and that is to make sure when I begin a project at home or set out to do something for myself, I complete it. I am easily distracted I have found, and though I always get these little things done, it may occur in fits and starts with big gaps in the middle. And this is not only with things that I DON'T want to do - like cleaning, putting away my laundry, filing papers....but even with things that I WANT to do.

So my take-away observation is that diligence is not only about school work and obligations to friends and the teams one plays on, it is about earnest care and effort in things that you do for YOU!
Have a good week.

Next up.......Be.....TUNED IN! I guess that probably doesn't mean turn on my radio, huh?
hahahaha

TUNED-IN

From: **Marny Jaastad** (marnymarie@yahoo.com)

To: evanmccleerybrown@yahoo.com

Date: Monday, March 11, 2013 3:48 AM

Hi Evan!

Be....tuned-in seems like it should be the overall theme for this little "experiment" I am doing. Or maybe project is a better word. Because with each word that I pick, I am driven to "tune in" to some aspect of the world or my life, or life in general and examine how that phrase is important and meaningful. But in and of itself, I took two things away from my "study" of being tuned-in. First, I realized that I am often not fully present and attentive when I am speaking with, or rather LISTENING TO, someone else talking. I found especially when I am listening to someone who tends to talk A LOT and who tends to tell long stories, I begin to think about other things.....what I am doing later; what's for dinner; what movies are out now; what is Evan doing today......my brain wanders. So I decided that everyone deserves for me to be tuned-in to them completely when we are talking or when I am working with them. Just as I would want someone to pay full attention to me when speaking it is important - even when someone may be a jabber-mouth - to give them your full attention. There may be something really interesting or useful that I can learn and use in my life that they may tell me at some point. Even if I may not be interested in, or even if I can't identify (with) 97% of what they say, SOME little part of it deems the whole thing worthy of 100% of my attention.

Second, it seems that there is also more going on than what people will actually divulge. But if you *tune in* to what may be an underlying message or an implied meaning in what someone says, you might take away a completely different understanding of what they are talking about. And sometimes though a person may say everything is fine, they are doing great, they have no problems or concerns, if you carefully observe their body language and the words that they *really* say, you can discern what they really are feeling without them saying it.

There are so many things that we can tune into in the world, every day, at school, practice, home, so much information passes by us all the time. I think it is very important that we are able to filter out everything else when we speak with each other and TUNE IN to their words and their feelings.

Hope you have a good week. Next up.......Be....FLEXIBLE. Oh boy this is gonna be my best challenge yet! I predict a lot of opportunity to put this (into) practice for me - it's a tough one in my life.

Love, Marny

FLEXIBLE

From: **Marny Jaastad** (marnymarie@yahoo.com)

To: evanmccleerybrown@yahoo.com

Date: Sunday, March 17, 2013 2:32 PM

Ok, first I am so psyched for you to have gotten into all of those schools! Nice to have so many choices! I will be very interested to see where you end up and how you come to that decision.
And now my "BEing" flexible......Like I said before this is a toughy for me because I make a plan or have something I want to do or do something in a certain way and I LIKE TO DO IT MY WAY! hahahha

So I challenged myself to be flexible this week by trying to generate several options or scenarios for how I might do a particular task or do my workout or train my clients. Instead of doing exactly what I would always do, I tried to watch other people to see how they did something or do my workout in reverse or at a different time of day.

Also, funnily enough, I also realized that I had changed around my meals a bit. Without being conscious of it, I just decided that I was bored of eating what I had been eating and just decided to try other things. But there ya go, being flexible!

My grand awakening about flexibility? HEY it just might make life less BORING! Instead of feeling like I was being inconvenienced or put upon when I needed to change a plan or negotiate with someone, I came to understand that here was an opportunity to do something differently - something I might like BETTER! Hey now imagine that. So now I have a few "new" things that I am doing during my week or my day.....hmmmm, wonder if I will be annoyed if and when one of them gets disrupted and I have to be flexible and change it! hahahaha

Love
Marny

Oh yah and new word to Be.....open-minded! Well that follows nicely from flexible! Let's see what I can un-earth with that!

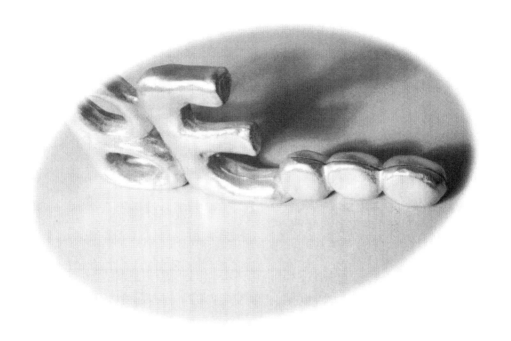

OPEN-
MINDED

From: **Marny Jaastad** (marnymarie@yahoo.com)

To: evanmccleerybrown@yahoo.com

Date: Sunday, March 23, 2013 6:03 PM

The one thing that is (as) certain as rain in Seattle in the winter is that I am a PLANNER. I plan every waking moment - and sometimes my sleeping ones too - to the tightest that I can. I plan ahead, I plan behind, I plan plan plan myself right into craziness and narrow-mindedness at times!

While I am *very* open minded in the traditional sense - gay marriage is fine, biracial couples are great, Jews are fabulous - I am not so open minded once I have A PLAN.

This week I challenged myself to unplan to an extent. When I find that I will have some extra time in my day, I tend to start making the list and the plan for how I will fill that time. And when it gets to the point in the day where I intend to do this big list, I often feel a sense of dread and obligation at having planned myself into it.

This week, when I had open time, I thought, "These are all the things I *could* do during that spare time. When it gets to that point, check in, see what you feel like and then either do 1 of the things you thought about .....or NOT."
And lo and behold what a great feeling to have not put so much pressure on myself to always accomplish some task or duty. I have so instilled in my brain that I must constantly be productive that I have begun to lose out on just "BE"ing at times. And being spontaneous. I forgot how to see many possibilities instead of only 1 path. How to decide it is ok to play, to do something for the pure joy of it.

I am sure that I will continue to plan plan plan. It is in my nature, and it does provide some level of comfort to feel in control of what will be going on. But I will also make a concentrated effort to let myself assess how I feel, what would make me feel good and then SCRAP THE PLAN if need be.
And now.....Be....creative! Ah yes. How FUN - and spontaneous!

Love, Marny

CREATIVE

Hi Evan

I will actually be hanging out with you in ONE LITTLE WEEK! Can't wait and I am very excited to hear about your school choice and the great programs it sounds like they have there.

I consider myself to be pretty creative, in general. I am not artistic or crafty, but I am very good (at) coming up with interesting gifts or fun workouts for my clients or nice greeting cards, etc. I also can be pretty creative when problem solving. My problems, clients' problems, friends' problems.........

Like the old saying goes, "feed me fish and I eat for a day, teach me how to fish and I eat for a lifetime"....I decided to work on helping *others* to be creative in problem solving. I am the type of person who likes to "fix" things for others. If someone presents a problem to me, I want to FIX IT NOW! That is a lovely sentiment but not necessarily always in the best interests of everyone.

What I have challenged myself with is to STOP when I want to immediately start to provide suggestions about how to: solve a problem, deal with a spouse/partner/friend, figure out a workout and eating plan, etc. and instead to ask the person questions to *guide them* toward (versus provide for them) a solution. This is a very big challenge for me as I do truly enjoy fixing - or at least thinking I can - problems for others. But if I can get them to start asking themselves questions and to parse out how they might approach the issues that come before them, then they will be much more successful in general in life.

I'll give you a report when I see you in a week as to my abilities at keeping my mouth shut! hahaha

Love, Marny

And for NEXT week, when I come to see you..........
BE...living your dreams!

How *perfect*!! one of my dreams is to be able to spend more time with you and your family so I know I am going to be able to accomplish this one from the get-go......we'll see what else crops up!
love, marny

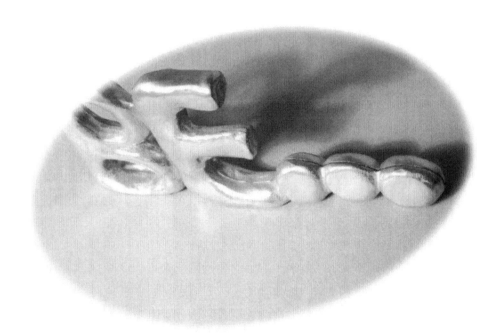

LIVING YOUR DREAMS

Subject: thank you again and BE...living your dreams

From: **Marny Jaastad** (marnymarie@yahoo.com)

To: evanmccleerybrown@yahoo.com

Date: Sunday, April 7, 2013 6:24 PM

So very very much for:
my earrings
letting me come to see you at school
hanging out with me - when you didn't have to!!
letting me have a great weekend w/ your family and you.

So I am going to keep BE...living your dreams on permanent display because it
will constantly remind me that there are things that I want to be doing
differently in life. AND it will make me ask myself...."What ARE my dreams?" I
think it is something we can ask ourselves every day.
I will write a little more later about "Be... living your dreams" but it will be a
work in progress, as life is.

Next up....BE.... thankful! HOW FUNNY IS THAT?!?!? Can't believe that I just
picked that one! Well I certainly will have plenty for which to be thankful when
I next write.
Love, Marny

Re: BE... living your dreams (part II)

From: **Marny Jaastad** (marnymarie@yahoo.com)

To: evanmccleerybrown@yahoo.com

Date: Friday, April 12, 2013 5:51 PM

Hi again

I didn't quite get to putting down all that I had thought about when I got back from seeing you and my week of pondering how to Be..living your dreams. So the big thing that struck me on the plane as I was being taken away from you all - which, by the way made me SO VERY SAD - was that we are only given one shot at this whole living your life thing. So you BETTER be living your dreams because you don't get a do-over!

I really had my eyes opened this weekend when I returned to San Diego and felt as though I WAS missing out on some things that I do truly consider to be my dreams. So I have begun to try to put into place those things that will allow me to be living the way that I want to - putting my dreams into reality.
The great thing is, dreams can always change. And I think that dreams can have stages or steps to them. There can be little dreams.....maybe school will be canceled today! And BIG DREAMS......maybe I will win the lottery!

What I also realized is that I am the Queen of Delayed Gratification. That means that I toil, and work and "suffer" and deny myself some pretty simple things merely because I feel like I must do certain things to EARN every little reward. Starting now that changes. Now I won't go crazy and start buying myself every single thing I see and say.....Awwww I LIKE that.

You can't be happy all the time and I don't expect to be. There are sad things that happen in life and there are obligations that we have to others and to ourselves, our school, job, family, friends. Step one is to realize and accept that we have dreams. Step two is to determine how realistic each might be (I am probably NOT going to make it to the Olympics in gymnastics in my life...haha). Step three is to formulate a plan to start to achieve those dreams.

This little "living your dreams" card will forever sit on my computer. It will not end up in the "discard" bag that I have collected the (other) cards in as I work through the ones in the little burlap bag of wisdom.

Thank you again for helping me come alive last weekend. Have fun and
remember to make a quest for (your) dreams.
Xoxo
Marny

THANKFUL

Hi Evan

Being thankful seems an easy task at first glance. I am thankful for so many things and people and opportunities in my life. I started to think about the different ways one might direct their thanks and gratitude.

First, the traditional, "thankfulness" for those things that I have - nice home, great family and friends, a job which provides me a good income and that I thoroughly enjoy. This I see as more in the sense of a spiritual or religious thankfulness. Like at Thanksgiving when everyone makes their "I am thankful for...." speech. This is very important, I think, on an annual or semi-annual basis to truly acknowledge those greater things in life that may be lost in the everyday shuffle and taken for granted.

Second there is being respectful and thankful in acknowledgement of some act of kindness or even a simple act of courtesy. This is more in the vein of having good manners. When you are five and learning to find your way in the world, and Mom says, "Make sure you say thank you to Charlie's mom for driving you home." She is teaching you how people learn to interact with each (other) in the world in a respectful and appropriate way.

But for ME, incorporating being thankful into my life as a practice is about finding and recognizing those things for which we do NOT thank people enough. The small things, the things that make life better every day, which many people don't even know they do for each other.

I used to make it a practice to write a thank you note to one of my clients every week for just "being them." I have not done this as much lately and I miss it and have vowed to re-institute this practice. It makes ME feel good and makes THEM feel *great*! I realize that they do not have to train at all, least of all with me. So for that I am certainly thankful. Or maybe they always walk in with a smile and a great attitude. Or they ask about my family or YOU or Wendy, my

44

silly cat. It's these small things that make each minute of every day a little better.

So I DID make a very concerted effort to tell a clerk in a store or my yoga teacher or a friend or a random stranger that they had done something that made my life better and to BE THANKFUL of and to them.
And *of course* I am ever so thankful that you provided me with this amazing gift which has allowed me to explore my life and the world around me in a different way every week or day or month.
Love, Marny

Woo hoo! I can't for this next one to unravel itself.....BE...FUN!!! Yay! I get to practice being silly and playful all week!

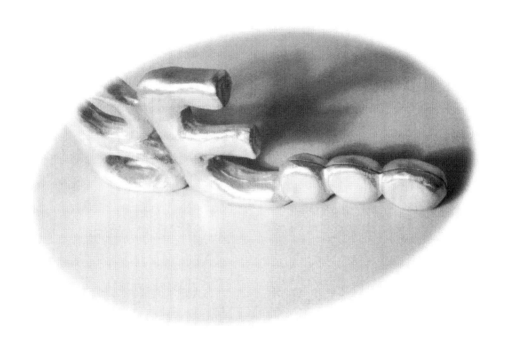

FUN

Ok so this was actually "FUN" in the end because I made it more of a brain game than a challenge to myself to BE... fun. Because I pretty much always try to make my clients' workouts fun and in general try to make people in my life feel good, have a good time and enjoy themselves, I think I can DO fun. Which is quite different than BEing fun.

What I really contemplated was WHY is fun so important in our lives? Yes, I know, that would seem quite obvious......well, because it's FUN! Right. But I started (to) watch and listen when people described something as fun or indicated that they had fun or wanted to have fun. And what I realized is that references to fun are inversely proportional to age......now what the heck can I mean by that?

Well as people get older, they use the word fun *more* often than when people are younger. So my theory on seeking fun is that it is an attempt at (re) capturing youth or even at making life more simple. Because in the end fun is really, purely simple. Even for you, compare yourself to Alex and how his life is so much more simple than yours. You now have obligations to school, family, teams, yourself. Sure Alex has homework sometimes and chores to do and a team to be a part of, BUT it is all pretty much fun most of the time. You however, now have things you know you have to do which are really not so much fun always. And then think about Mom and Dad and me and how many things we do that might not be so much fun. And so I think that FUN for adults is about making life simple again, about going back to being 7 or even younger when you could sit in the backyard for hours til Mom said to come in for dinner and be completely entertained by the birds and worms and mud and sticks and leaves and trees and whatever else existed in nature and just BE.... fun.

My new outlook on fun is to see what I can let go of in terms of scheduling things for myself and being rigid about my workouts and my day in general. When something grabs my attention for some reason of interest and seems like it might bring me some joy and happiness, then I will do my very best to allow myself to step away from my adult, scheduled life and soak in all the fun. Fun, for me, will come from spontaneity and simple-ness. Hope you have a really FUN week.

Love, Marny
Next up............BE compassionate.   Stay tuned!

COMPASSIONATE

Subject: Be...compassionate

From: **Marny Jaastad** (marnymarie@yahoo.com)

To: evanmccleerybrown@yahoo.com

Date: Monday, April 29, 2013 3:35 AM

HI!

Oh this is a toughy for me! There are times when it is very, very easy to be compassionate - for a person or situation that is particularly difficult; to dismiss bad behavior when someone is under a great deal of stress; feeling sympathy for someone's loss of a loved one. There are other times, however, when I found myself quite challenged this week to feel compassion for someone who was in a painful or difficult situation.

Example one: man next to me in yoga with a HORRIBLE head cold.......well, at least that BETTER have been the excuse he had for making all the noise he made. I wanted to hand him my towel and tell him to blow his nose! (And keep the towel). I kept trying, *really really trying!!* to feel badly for this man. But honestly all I could get to was wondering if he might have the compassion to leave the class so the rest of us could relax a bit. So I admit, I have failed on that count. I am sorry that he felt badly and I am sure that he thought doing some exercise might clear up his head and get things moving - well that it did. Unfortunately I had to listen to and be a little sickened by the sounds.....ugh

So I did keep trying and there were a couple of times when I really did step up and show some compassion when I might otherwise have been cynical or less than caring.

Yesterday brought me a completely random opportunity to be compassionate for, or at least to take pity on someone......I went to the gym to go to work later in the day, since I had run a 1/2 marathon in the a.m. I parked on the street in front of the gym and as I made a u-turn to park there I noticed something in the road. I thought it was a glasses case or a makeup bag or a piece of cloth. I almost left it and started to walk into the gym then turned around, ran into the street and grabbed.........someone's wallet! This woman's entire life was in this wallet. Everything: credit cards, driver license, auto club cards, cash, receipts,

50

business cards. Everything, that is except for a personal phone number. So I called the business phone where I left a message - that I knew no one would get until Monday a.m. and I kept thinking how much she must be panicking. I then called her 24 hour roadside assistance card and told them the story and hoped they would be able to contact her. Finally by evening, through a couple of us trying, we were able to find a home phone by searching online and got through to her! She was ecstatic of course and said she had been shopping in the mall next door and must have set the wallet on top of her car as she put her daughter in the car.......drove off and WHOOOOSH! flew off the car.

So more a good deed than compassion, but picking up the wallet, I became really invested in trying to alleviate the pain and aggravation that I knew she must be going through and so I am going to call this my official act of compassion for the week! hahaha
Love , Marny

Next up.......BE...HAPPY! OH YAH! No problemo there. I can already say that since this 1/2 marathon is done, I am ECSTATIC. Forget happy. So today will be a super day. I ought to be able to get enough happy in the next 3 days for an entire week!

AN EMAIL
FROM EVAN

Subject: gifts

From: evanmccleerybrown@yahoo.com

To: **Marny Jaastad** (marnymarie@yahoo.com)

Date: Tuesday, April 30, 2013 3:21 PM

Dear Marny,

Thank you for all the wonderful gifts you have gotten me in the past few weeks. I love the Axe Apollo. It makes me smell me great everyday. I also like the Lakeside bag. It is great because I now have something that will represent me in my new school. I also love the business cards for Sports news junior. I'm going to give them to everybody! I'm reading all your emails about the Be.....I enjoy reading them even if I don't respond.

Hope things are going well down in San Diego. How's Wendy?

Love,

Evan

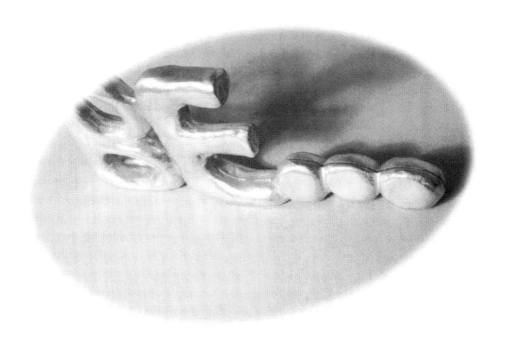

HAPPY

From: **Marny Jaastad** (marnymarie@yahoo.com)

To: evanmccleerybrown@yahoo.com

Date: Sunday, May 5, 2013 5:10 PM

Hey Ev!

This was easy peasy! Every time I was doing something that I thought that I really didn't want to do, I said to myself BE HAPPY! At least you: have a job (even if I don't always want to be there); have a strong, healthy body (even though it is tired sometimes); have a beautiful house even if I do sometimes have to clean it and do regular maintenance on it.

So I tried to notice when I was feeling grumpy or less than happy and told myself in my head "Be happy!" It immediately changed my mood and my actual feeling, inside and out. I just felt better. No other way to describe it. And I found this to be the case more so than with any of the other phrases or words that have come before this. So I wondered what it is about being happy/finding happiness that is so important to all of us and what I surmised is that being happy purely and simply feels GOOD. You hear people say "I am not happy with my job, my relationship, my performance....." And why do we not like that? Because it is just no fun to NOT be happy. Too bad we can't achieve it all the time. I guess if we were never UNhappy, we would not be able to so enjoy or appreciate happiness when we are in it.

It reminded me of a book I read recently called *The Geography of Bliss*. So this author went all over the world, to various countries trying to determine the origins of happiness, what creates happiness......money, security, love.......what he finally sums up with is:
"Money matters, but less than we think and not in the way that we think. Family is important. So are friends. Envy is toxic. So is excessive thinking. Beaches are optional. Trust is not. Neither is gratitude."
I buy into it all I think. But mostly I like it. Simple, happy. And I keep it on a piece of paper above my desk.

So I hope that you have a VERY happy week and thank you again so much for making me happy just when I think of you!

Next up.......BE...STRONG. Uh oh, I sense that I will have some challenges coming my way this week and I will have to have mental strength. I actually DID set my intention in my yoga class today to bring me STRENGTH from the class so there ya go! I'm off and running with it already.

Love, Marny

STRONG

Hi Evan!

Sorry it's been a little bit. I had a quick trip out of town and it threw my whole schedule off. Not a bad thing, as the trip was great but it left me catching up and not able to do some of the things that I really LIKE to do - like writing to you. Being strong is such an amorphous idea. Obviously there is physical strength, which for some people, might be something that they do need to focus on. But for you and me and your family, the meaning of being strong has more to do with mental fortitude and perseverance, maybe even patience. "Stay the course" "Don't lose your focus" "Stiff upper lip" were all phrases that came to mind for me when I pondered Be...Strong.

I have a lot of challenges and changes coming my way this year. And whether you think you do or not, I thought about you as well and all of the changes YOU have coming - new school, friends, routine. Tough stuff. Sometimes it is easiest to just put your head in the sand, pull the blankets over your head and stay in bed. But we don't, we remain strong, we carry on, we persevere. A lot of that comes from our families

I also very often have to be strong *for others*. Now there's an interesting thought - having mental fortitude for others. But so often the burdens of our lives are too great for us alone that we rely on the shoulders of others to help us carry our troubles. It can be exhausting to not only support yourself but to have to keep a fair portion of your mental strength available to others whenever they may need it.

For me being strong over the next year will mean having perspective - I will need to maintain the big picture in my mental mirror. There is a lot of great stuff that I am trying to foster into coming to life and to venture out some new ways in my life. To be...living my dreams, as we already explored. And change always requires mental focus and will. To want the change, to see the change, to create the change and to accept the change. Whew. I'm already tired just thinking about it! However, I have YOU to thank for launching some of that change and though you may not know it, I draw strength from YOU as well. Thank you for your strength and for helping me, through this wonderful (though seemingly so simple) gift, to test my strength and to BE!

Love you to the moon,
Marny

INVOLVED

Be...involved

From: **Marny Jaastad** (marnymarie@yahoo.com)

To: evanmccleerybrown@yahoo.com

Date: Sunday, May 26, 2013 8:07 AM

Hi Ev!

Wellllll there were so many angles from which this concept/word/action came at me this week it is almost laughable. Be involved, I thought.......ok, take an interest in the world, engage my clients about their "worlds" (which I really do all the time anyway), don't be a passive observer letting life pass you by.......And those were all true to some extent but I had two pretty big ones that in retrospect made me realize how important it is to BE...INVOLVED.

It's very easy for me to be involved in the lives of my clients. Each session is very often more therapy - mental - then therapy - physical. As a consequence, I know a lot about a lot of people in this little town of ours. And I know how many of their lives intertwine and meet. Sometimes, being involved can put me in some very interesting - read: DIFFICULT - positions. But my clients know that I am a steel trap. What goes into my ears and brain, stays there. No one finds out - well except maybe Wendy when I come home and say "you will never believe this..." And sometimes Mom because I have to have someone help me process some of the things that people tell me. Because I choose to take that role on - being an integral part of many people's lives, there is a responsibility of owning up to that as well. Of being discreet, supportive, checking back to make sure they are doing ok. And I really enjoy that part of my job the most. I like to help people. Period. In any way I can.

Being involved in the world is a larger, broader, more diffuse concept. I like to think that I try to remain informed and aware of what is going on all over the world, or even in my local area. And while I am generally quite up-to-date on whatever "the news" is, I do not find that I particularly involve myself in it in terms of trying to affect or take a stance on what may be occurring. I think that's ok with me for now. Not everyone is meant to be political or vocal about the greater issues in the world. BUT if you are passionate about something, then it is important that you be involved with it and try to affect whatever change or outcome you would like to see with it. Even if that is lobbying your family about something that you would like to do for free time or a family trip, etc. BEing INVOLVED in your own life, not simply letting it pass you by as if you were only along for the ride.

The event that I now realize in retrospect was all about being involved happened last Friday. My dad and stepmom were visiting me for the long Memorial Day Weekend and I was working on Friday morning until about 10. I had planned to do my usual Friday 2 hour run and then sneak in a yoga class that I never get to take because I usually have clients. When I finished my work at about 9.30, I sat and thought "What the heck are you thinking planning to go exercise for 3 hours while you could have that precious time spent with people who traveled 1/2 way across the country to see you and whom you adore!" And so I decided to BE INVOLVED with my family, the people I love, and to NOT be SELF-involved, and I texted dad to see where they were and surprised them at the coffee shop, (riding up) on my bike. We went on a beautiful, long hike that afternoon and I was thrilled and <u>proud</u> of myself for making the decision. It is so easy for me, and I think for most of us to be SELF-involved most of the time. The world is bigger than we are and sometimes ME has to take a backseat to US.

It's actually pretty amazing to see what differences can occur in the world, your life, or even 1 simple minute in the day if you act, participate, INVOLVE yourself in the moment, the act, the decision, the direction of this world, this life that we have only 1 chance to test out.

And on this Memorial Day Weekend, I choose to involve myself in the lives of my family and your family. From today forward, BE...INVOLVED has a new meaning for me.

love, Marny

I may just have exhausted myself cogitating on all of this. Think maybe I'll NOT be involved in any big decisions for the rest of the day. Maybe I'll just sit back and let the world pass me by. HAHAHA

Next up........BE...FIRED UP! Oh YEAH!!!!!!!!!! I am going to be the cheerleader of the century this week!

FIRED-UP

From: **Marny Jaastad** (marnymarie@yahoo.com)

To: evanmccleerybrown@yahoo.com

Date: Saturday, June 1, 2013 6:09 PM

Hellloooo EVAN!

Woo hoooo! How's that for a start?? Fired UP! Well, usually. Some days it's really tough, I have found. But what I really tried to remember is that the energy I can put out into the universe - at work, in play, with family, with friends, to random strangers really does manifest itself in a continuation of that energy and FIRED UP-ness. So every morning I have been trying to fire myself up - little pep talks, little gems of incentive I can look forward to throughout the day, SOME thing that makes putting my feet on the floor and getting out of bed just a little more worth it......

Shoot! I AM fired up. Or at least extremely motivated and now extremely tired. I pretty much hit the ground running on Tuesday a.m. and haven't stopped since. I knew I was going to have a week or so of "catch up" because I had my dad and stepmom here for 5 days over the Memorial Day Weekend. And I was right! It's nice to know that you can ramp it up when need be and put your head down and really get stuff done.....when you KNOW there's an end in sight!

I think getting fired up is a lot more important as we get older than when we are younger. In RETROSPECT of course, it is easy for me to say that "As a kid/young person/young adult it's easy to get fired up. Life is simple. How hard could it be to get fired up?" Wellllll I actually thought about that weekend I went to see you and how you and Alex and Jaden and Hayden had to play all of your games in THE RAIN!!! And I *know* that is not a good time yet you guys all stepped up and got yourselves FIRED UP to play.

Now here's the tricky part about being fired up.........when do you cross the line and become just plain manic and annoying? Can you be TOO fired up? As I mulled this over while in yoga tonight - yes, I know you are NOT supposed to think in yoga....too bad, I did! Anyway I mulled it over and decided that YES, in fact, one can be too fired up. There IS an edge that one must not fall over in having enthusiasm and excitement for something. That crossover point is what

64

lands some people in that truly irritating and horrible position of being way too excited. I have encountered numerous individuals who fall decidedly into this category over the years. Their passion possesses them and turns them into "that person I can't wait to get away from."

It had never really occurred to me that one could actually be too fired up. Kinda like when Mom has 1 too many coffees and looks like a whirling dervish. Well sort of but not quite. I am not exactly sure how one might prevent oneself from falling over the edge into the Pit of Zealousness but I am guessing based on observation that these people have always been this way - from day 1. Out of the womb and straight into walking and talking 100 miles an hour.

Life really is a matter of fine lines, if you think about it. Each and every positive thing that we may try to emulate or build into our daily practice can be taken that 1 step too far, *past* the tipping point rather than perfectly balancing on it. I think this may actually be my observation over the next few weeks. Whatever my BE is next, I am going to look at that balance. Can there be too much BE? hmmmmmm

Ok, next up for the judgment of what is the perfect amount to BE...INSPIRED! Well. I think that maybe I just was, so I am already off to a PHENOMENAL start! Wow, I could go anywhere with this inspired thing.......or not....that may be a bit too much fired-up-ness.

Love, Marny
And I am about to go into 1 month countdown mode til I see you again! Now THAT gets me FIRED UP!

INSPIRED

Subject: Be...inspired!

From: **Marny Jaastad** (marnymarie@yahoo.com)

To: evanmccleerybrown@yahoo.com

Date: Monday, June 10, 2013 3:36 AM

Dear Evan,

I was obviously kidding about being inspired about being fired up. But it was a nice segue anyway. However, I had a small inspiration today. At least I think I can categorize it that way. I was walking to my car after going to coffee with a friend and we came up behind a man and woman with a LOT of groceries and the woman (had) a baby in a carrier on her tummy. They had all four of their arms full and I noticed that one of the guy's bags was ripping and he was going to lose..........HIS COFFEE!! OH NO! hahaha. So I stopped them and told them (the bag was breaking) and they put everything down and tried to re-shuffle.......As I approached my car I thought, "DUH I have a ton of fabric shopping bags in the car." So I grabbed one and ran back to them and said, "Put everything in here. I have a million bags." They just looked at me dumbfounded and thankful. It made my day! INSPIRATION.

The other thing I was thinking about this inspiration stuff is to observe what inspires others - to act or to *not* act - in particular situations. I have spent the first 1/3 of this little project (yes, we are 1/3 through the 72 BE's) focusing on ME and what I observe about BEing. So now I am going to ask others about their inspirations - in life, in general. I will in particular listen to when people actually use the phrase "that inspired me" or something to that effect.......let's see what BE...inspired might bring to light in others.

And so I watched people and ....What a lovely inspiration I had the other day. I observed someone do something COMPLETELY selfless and wholly generous for someone else. There was a latecomer to a class I was in. Everyone was already in their "spot" and when this person came in they wanted a spot next to a wall but there was a person already in that place. That person happened to be a staff member so she knew the latecomer and knew that she had "preferences" for where she liked to be in class. The woman did ask her to move and without a thought she picked up her things - though class had already started - and moved right up front, as there was nowhere else to go. I was totally inspired by her generosity and completely selfless act. As I thought about it afterwards, I realized that I was first: irritated with the person for coming late knowing full well that she likes to have a specific place to be (and that she brings a lot of "gear" with her) and second: observing about myself that though I likely would have moved, I would have been very resentful of having to do so and it would have clouded my entire class........SO I was inspired - after the fact and after thinking more about it - by this woman who without a 2nd thought or any malice, graciously allowed an intrusion into her space. Funny how you have to turn your mind over sometimes to see what might have been OR more importantly what could be in the future. It will be interesting to see if I am ever in a situation like this again how I will react. I can only hope that I will be as gracious and selfless and NOT AT ALL resentful in being able to allow others to make errors and to forgive them those errors.

At the end of all of this what I have actually concluded is that people say "that inspires me" or "how inspirational" or some other form of claiming to BE....inspired. But what truly does that mean? What I now believe is that people merely state they are inspired by something but by the definition according to MARNY, what should then follow is some action which is reflective of that inspiration. Next time someone says that they were inspired by or about or as a result of something, I am going to ask them WHAT it was exactly that they were inspired to DO. What action did they take as a result of what they witnessed or read or heard as "inspiring"? I think that we talk too much and do too little as a population. And I am going to be INSPIRED to get people DOing again!

love and inspiration,
Marny

REFLECTIVE

From: **Marny Jaastad** (marnymarie@yahoo.com)

To: evanmccleerybrown@yahoo.com

Date: Monday, June 17, 2013 3:41 AM

Dear Evan

Life can be funny sometimes.....as you read through this you may laugh. Talk about coming full-circle. In the end, I got "reflected" TO this week as I was trying to BE....reflective. I worked so hard at being a mirror (to others) that I bounced some of it right back to myself. How convenient!

Instead of starting to BE reflective this week, I began by asking WHY do we want to be reflective? WHY do we look back over lives/choices/days/events and rehash them? Aren't we always told to look forward, don't look back, move ahead. Yes, but we are also told to learn from our mistakes, remember history or you will be doomed to repeat it. Hmmmmm, opposite but equally valuable admonitions.

I believe that being reflective is about not being *regretful*. People reflect back upon something to ensure and cement in their belief that they have done/been/acted well and in the way that would bring them the greatest good or happiness.

WELL! Now let's see where that thought takes me this week. As I reflect upon it (HA!) as well as my life/choices/events/week/day/hour of the past......
NOW I have really outdone myself.......I have decided: I am going to be like a mirror - REFLECTIVE- to other people. I am going to send back to them what they send to me......especially the good stuff. And the "bad" stuff I will try to send back in a way that helps to eliminate the bad stuff. Oh this could be a great game!

Who ever thought that BE...reflective could be a forward looking type (of) thing and not actually (be about) looking back at all. More (so) being in the moment with people and helping them to recognize what they are putting out to the world. As people get older, I have observed that they are far less self-aware of their outward emotions/energy/attitudes than they are when younger AND more importantly than OTHERS are aware of......I am very guilty of this. I know because I have been told that I seem "angry", unfriendly, scary...many things that I am NOT and that I certainly do not want to portray or put out to the world. So I am going to work on being reflective back to others about what they are sending out - in a subtle, not cruel or in-your-face way. With this tactic, maybe I can help to foster a little more self-awareness and harmony among everyone. We should all learn to be like a mirror - reflective!

Watch some of the adults you encounter over the next few weeks and see if you observe what I have observed. Could be interesting.....or NOT! And maybe you can hone your mirror skills and send back either the positive things that they are sending out or help them to recognize what they may be sending out inadvertently and unintentionally. Maybe you too can be reflective for them.

And in one final "P.S" to (this) week's mental mirror......just yesterday a friend sat me down and reflected me back to me! HAH! Well what comes around goes around - literally. Though it was valuable personally, it was also quite interesting to gain the experience and insight that I had been trying to deliver to others. Whomever is directing the grand play that is Our Lives must have gotten quite a chuckle out of my personal quid pro quo!

Love Marny

Getting closer to seeing you! Only a few more weeks. If you think about it over that time, let me know which of the "BE's" has been your favorite so far.

And now we are going to BE...INFORMED! This already gives me all kinds of ideas.....

INFORMED

Subject: Be...informed

From: **Marny Jaastad** (marnymarie@yahoo.com)

To: evanmccleerybrown@yahoo.com

Date: Sunday, June 23, 2013 5:18 PM

Happy Summer Solstice Sunday!

The *very* first thing that came to my mind about being informed: don't act
hastily. I know that I am well-read, up-to-date on job-related things and
interested in current events. However, I was intrigued that the idea of getting
all the facts and info before jumping to conclusions/making decisions or
evaluations popped up first in my head. Hm. Well I did not personally have
occasion to BE...informed about making a specific decision this week, I WAS able
to offer that advice to several other people who, ironically enough, asked my
opinion on something that was going on in their lives to which they were
reacting quite strongly. I laughed (to myself) and said....maybe it is not all what
it seems and you need to investigate further before making a rash decision or
taking an action that you might regret. And in at least one of the cases, it was a
very good thing that the individual DID ask a few more questions and get
informed a little more on the situation as the events were not as they had
originally appeared and she could have very well destroyed a friendship. So
chalk one up to Marny for being The Wise Sage. That really only comes from
having erred myself quite a few times and letting my own hot head get the
better of my rational brain. Ah yes, to live and to learn, the quintessential piece
of advice.

BUT I did decide just today that what I MUST become more informed about is
ME. And by that I mean I have been feeling a little out of sorts and not quite
fitting into the current mold that I am living in. However, I have not been able
to see a path or my way toward something that might find me more happiness,
peace and a feeling of providing true value and worth to other people. SO my
task now is to BE...informed about ME; about what is really going on in my head
in terms of my likes, dislikes and dreams and wishes for the future. How will I
get there? What do I want it to look like? WHEW! Big questions. Gee I always
thought when I grew up I would know that I had arrived......apparently growing
up is not an end but a continual evolution. Sorry to lay that on you at the age of
(almost!) 12...... I can tell you though that it gets *easier* in a relative sense, at

least, to grow up. Maybe only because the distance to travel becomes shorter and all of those wonderful people in our lives who offer "advice" (like me!) make our mental encyclopedia vast and plentiful.

BE...informed always before deciding your next step, weigh every option available and choose the one most suited to you at that particular time. That is *not* to say choose the "best" alternative. Choose what your heart says is your path and your way based upon the information you have.
Love, Marny

We are next going to BE...YOUR BEST! Well I already know that YOU are your very best always. And I believe that this follows beautifully with my own quest to be informed about myself so that I may be MY VERY BEST!!!!

YOUR
BEST

From: **Marny Jaastad** (marnymarie@yahoo.com)

To: evanmccleerybrown@yahoo.com

Date: Sunday, June 30, 2013 4:21 PM

Hey Evan

Well this topic seems appropriate today, as Mom just told me you had a rough game and I KNOW you did YOUR BEST! Anyway, onto my thoughts on what it might mean in the general world to BE... your best.

What a seemingly simple and may I even say obvious "BE." Who wouldn't want to be their best every day in every way? Ok, well yes some people don't really give one whit about being their best. Being soso or not even all that good is just plain fine with them. BUT for the majority of us, I would put forth that one's "best" is a relatively universal pursuit. Yet, that phrase may also be overused to some extent. And as with anything, overuse can lead to (the) dilution of purity of something. It has lost some of its true impact and meaning. Coaches, teachers, parents, teammates, friends, the list could go on ad infinitum as to who uses these simple words to encourage us to achieve and to *succeed*. And succeed is the word I am identifying with as the reason I feel overuse (of "your best") has led to a change in the true essence of "your best." Do you always succeed when you do your best? Does "failure" indicate one did NOT do one's best?

Perfect case in point for me this week. This year I had decided that I would not work as many hours as I had in the past. It was way too much and I was tired and unhappy and cranky. But it has been very tough, mentally, for me to not make as much money and feel like I am being a slacker! It's silly because I am still the busiest trainer in the gym and haven't started to eat cat food yet so I am completely supporting myself. BUT am I doing my best I ask myself? Because I KNOW I have worked a lot more and made a lot more in previous years. I often feel guilty or as though I am lazy because I am not at that same level. HOWEVER, I do know that I was NOT "BEing....my best" in terms of what I was providing to my clients. I was often in a grumpy mood - though it never showed to them as anything more than being quiet. And I feel like the sessions I have now are much more personal and a better experience for them. It's not an assembly line job and that is how I had begun to treat it. Hmmmm, I continue to ponder this one as it is a difficult spot for me to be in.

And maybe most importantly, <u>who</u> possesses the right to define FOR YOU what is "your best"??? Now therein lies the true meaning and value of BE...your best. If you are to be YOUR best, then by definition, should it not be YOUR right alone to outline and determine what that "best" you is? I am actually a little uncertain myself as to whom should possess the ability to define for each of us what our best in any given situation may be. We have inside perspective looking out but others have outside perspective (and possibly broader experiences) from which to draw an accurate depiction (of) OUR BEST.

And lo and behold I had the very experience I describe above - WHO defines my best - this week as well. Gee - opportunity to expound on "your best" was everywhere this week. My boss made a small comment one day about how another trainer was "close on my heels" for bringing in revenue this month and it TOTALLY caught my attention. And he is no dumb bunny, I know he wanted it to catch my attention. The next day I totally stepped up and got a huge amount of revenue into our club by really going over my accounts and getting people to buy more sessions. I knew, in retrospect, that I had been slacking off from what I could be doing.......and just needed that little nudge to push me forward again. I appreciated his push and I appreciated the opportunity to LEARN from this little gem about BEing...YOUR BEST!

I know in your game tomorrow you will be at YOUR very best. Regardless of the outcome, I know the passion and energy and focus that you put into all that you do and that makes me very, very proud. You are simply MY BEST thing in life to know and watch grow up!

Love, Marny

Can't wait to see you!
AND for this week, that we will get to be together......I will be musing over.........BE...PRODUCTIVE! Well, I've got stuff to do now for work tomorrow, so let's get it done and I will start right now with being productive!

PRODUCTIVE

Be...productive

From: **Marny Jaastad** (marnymarie@yahoo.com)

To: evanmccleerybrown@yahoo.com

Date: Thursday, July 11, 2013 3:39 AM

Hi Evan and Happy Continuing Summer (which may be the antithesis of BE... productive but is certainly a necessary time in life).......

How easy it is these days - well, you wouldn't know "these days" from other days - BUT it is soooooo easy now to while away time online or on any screens......wow talk about a productivity sucker. It's like going down Alice's rabbit hole and going and going. You can just dig deeper and deeper into the Web and get sucked all over the place looking and looking and definitely NOT being productive.

I will be productive this week, as I need to cram in a whole bunch before (I) come to see YOU! I'd like to think that I am always being productive. Somewhat by the nature of my job, I am generally productive all day long. Whenever I am with a client, I am "producing".....what exactly? Well, health, happiness (I hope, after a bit of pain!), longevity, good habits. In the best of all possible situations (and if I want to really boost my ego) I am producing longer life! Gee, I can pump myself up pretty well extolling the virtues of my productivity!

Now I do know full well the one place that I tend to be very UNproductive. That is taking care of the general maintenance and upkeep issues in my home. I can find MANY MANY MANY other things to do than to: vacuum, scrub, polish, dust, clean, put away and be productive in my spare time. Hmmmm, spare time. Now that's a concept that seems at odds with productivity. Should I strive to be productive during spare time - or maybe productivity is measured in different ways. Maybe in NOT being productive and taking some down, mindless, "wasted" time, one actually is able to re-boot and to be even more productive when called upon to do so. The ever-present slippery slope theory however, comes into play here as it might become quite easy to justify laziness and idleness by claiming the rejuvenating effects are required for some future use.......For myself, there exists an internal "guilt" meter which allows me to essentially fart away some indistinct amount of time doing not much of anything

- cruising the web, thumbing through a clothing catalog, searching for coooool gifts for coooool people - before it goes off in my head and says, "Hey, you've really gotta get some stuff done now, lady."

And productivity pervades our society. As I said above, summer break is a necessary time in every child's life. A break from school, rigorous schedules and endless routine. But even then, what is the first thing our parents say as we roll out of bed on the First Day of Summer....."You are not going to sit around and do NOTHING all summer so figure out what you want to do." Basically - BE...productive!

We just can't ever escape that internal drive to DO. Something. Anything. No idleness. Probably comes from that (phrase) "idle hands being the devil's workshop" or something like that.

Well now that I've expounded at not so great a length of time about being productive, the clock ticks and I must get ready for work so that I can be verrrry productive today. Maybe I'll even get out the dust rag and vacuum cleaner when I get home tonight......or NOT!
xoxox Marny

We are onto BE...patient. Well what a lovely challenge for me this week. And maybe for you as well, as you anticipate getting ready to go to Maine.

Oh yippee! Not my strongest point. Good thing I didn't draw this past week when I was waiting to come to see you. I would definitely have failed that "BE" mission.

PATIENT

Subject: Be...patient (UGH!)

From: **Marny Jaastad** (marnymarie@yahoo.com)

To: evanmccleerybrown@yahoo.com

Date: Friday, July 19, 2013 5:09 PM

Hey Evan! Happy Maine - well almost - are you IMpatient about getting there yet???? hahahaha

Ok I'll put it right out there up front. I HATE ABHOR DETEST being patient. That said, it is likely one of the very *best* things that I can try to BE. So I am up to the challenge and will promise myself to be aware of impatience with myself, others and the world at large.

Wow what a week of patience and NON patience. I actually thought a great deal about this one. Lots of different things floated through my mind. I think I may end up keeping this out for continued rumination and possibly Part II of BE....patient!

Here were the first few things that flew through my mind - and mostly continued to circulate there as well -

First, I pondered the difference between patient in a hospital and being patient - WHY are those the same word???? The original/Latin meaning is "one who suffers"......well yes, that would be true in both cases I guess. But then if "patience is a virtue" it must follow that SUFFERING is a virtue? I would argue NOT! However, if "good things come to those who wait" then I am onboard for that. Suffering leading to good things....HA! I can see it but when is it worth all that pain? (The mental of course not the physical, of the anguish of waiting). Which leads me to....why is it so gosh-darn, fundamentally HARD to BE PATIENT??? Even babies and animals seem to possess the "be Impatient" (trait). You ever try to ignore a crying baby or worse to walk past a *hungry* Tucker and not be inundated with cries or barks or howls or dog underfoot?

It was really brought home to me about how impatient I am as I made several BIG decisions this week about changing some things going on in my life so that I would be happier and BE...living my dreams (as I told you, that one sits on my computer all the time). Anyway, I have been mulling over and perseverating about finding some new opportunities for work, play, life, etc. And I had found myself really stuck - not moving anywhere forward and not able to see the path I even wanted to take. Then BAM I had a very, very challenging day one day this week and in one day, did FOUR BIG things that could have the potential to bring me closer to that ever-elusive "BE"...living my dreams. So what I realized is that I often do take a long time to figure out what I want to do in a particular situation. I think and make notes and think some more and research and then FINALLY come to a decision and ACT on it. However, the problem arises that in my head, everything is said and done and the changes should be immediate, as in right NOW, because I am ready RIGHT NOW. Ummmm, sadly the world does not work that way. So! My patience is currently being tested as I sit and wait for responses to a couple of things that involve other people and organizations.

Well, good things come to those who wait, right?!?!? I am practicing my good yoga and breathing, trying to be "in the moment" and letting everything come at me without judgement. BUT could it all just hurry up and get here so I can get a move on with my new life?!??! Sheeeesh, I just don't want to BE....patient!

Lots of love, hope this made you laugh a little. I actually could picture you several times in the past when you have been really, really excited to do something and you just really, really, really did NOT want to wait......It makes me smile and laugh that we share a common bond of IMpatience!
Marny

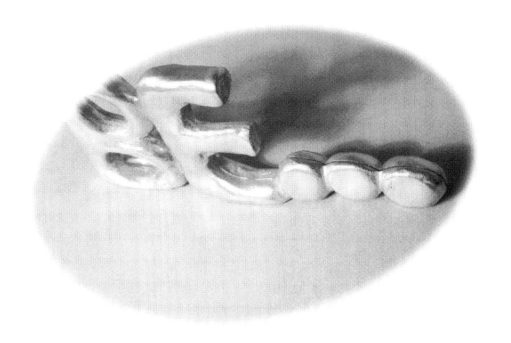

GOOD TO
YOURSELF

Subject: Be...good to yourself!

From: **Marny Jaastad** (marnymarie@yahoo.com)

To: evanmccleerybrown@yahoo.com

Date: Friday, August 2, 2013 5:12 PM

Hey Big 12 year old, I'm almost a teenager and will never talk to Marny again Guy! (LOL)

I seriously do hope that your birthday was rock star caliber - especially Boston and Sox game. At first I felt pretty unattached to "BE...good to yourself." Yah yah yah....whatever. Pat yourself on the back once in a while; don't get down on yourself when you make a mistake; be ok with giving yourself a "treat" and not feel guilty! BUT then......(as always with these wonderous little words and phrases) my mind began to dig into it more deeply.

Wow - this could not have come up at a more perfect time. I have been very hard on myself and giving myself a lot of grief and negative head-talk lately because I have wanted to make changes in my life but have not been able to muster the initiative to do so. (As I said in last week's BE...patient, I DID actually muster it. All in 1 day which was a little overwhelming; but necessary in retrospect). Since then I have tried to be a little softer - for lack of a better word - with myself. It's tough though as I am forever feeling as though I am not measuring up, that I need to raise my bar of performance. If I can do "X" 1 week I should be able to do 2 times "X" the following week. Now of course this is an unreasonable expectation but I make it nonetheless and if I cannot achieve 2 times "X" I mentally berate myself and punish myself in some way. Silliness and not very useful in any way.

Now is the perfect time for me to BE...good to me. I am pretty darn good to everyone else so here's my challenge to turn that intention INWARDS and see what I can do for little ole me.

What I finally did come to conclude is that being good to me has really meant not putting my decisions on hold or by the wayside for the what if's of others. Opting for what I want to do, versus harboring concern that someone else might possibly need or want my services/presence in lieu of some other plan I have. Case in point - INDEPENDENCE DAY! And how aptly named for me this year. I came to visit all of you. Such a *simple* act. Something people do alllll the time - visit those that they love. BUT never before in the 10 years that I have been in my job have I left the gym during the summer months for ANY vacation. I always said, "Oh I can't. We're so busy. My clients....." But THIS year, in large part due to YOU and this amazing gift of reflection and challenge that you have provided, I said, "Darn it all! I am doing what I want to do!" And guess what? The world did not end, clients did not disappear, I am not broke and I had one of the best times of my life being with all of you. Simply being a part of your life for a few days.

Taking other people's *feelings* into account when making your life choices is very important, but not necessarily taking their actions - which may or may not include you - into account. And there we have BE...good to yourself. Put you first sometimes, be ok with it, and then revel in it; never regret it. I have learned one big thing in life - most people are really only concerned with themselves. Very few of us put "them" before "me". So if you and I don't put "us" first, who else will?!?!?

Love love love you
Marny

And.....number 31 in the BE series is..........just for #31 Kameron Loe.....BE...FOCUSED! How awesome is THAT for a baseball analogy!?!?!

FOCUSED

Be...focused!!!

From: **Marny Jaastad** (marnymarie@yahoo.com)

To: evanmccleerybrown@yahoo.com

Date: Sunday, August 11, 2013 2:24 PM

Hi Evan! I hope that this makes you laugh and I hope maybe you can identify with this one a little more than the others and send some pity my way! (haha) Oh puuuuhleeeze! I am the Queen of Focus!!!! Are you kidding?!?!? If there is 1 thing that people have said about me over many, many, many years it is that I am always SO FOCUSED! So.....what can I learn about BE...focused.....

Ohhh OK NOW I get it.........I actually called myself out on this one.....
Yup I'm a focused gal on SOME things. BUT I am the biggest culprit of MULTI-TASKING. Yes, the ever-popular activity wherein one *believes* that one is actually accomplishing a whole lot of stuff when in reality - as studies have shown - each of those things does not get done well, or well-done, at all. I had to be very focused on something last weekend - a 3-plus hour test! Yes, really 3 hours. And I could have used more. Ugh 230 questions, mostly written, not a/b/c or true/false. I was completely immersed in that test and nothing else even occurred to me over the 3 hours. (Which by the way FLEW by). It came to me on Monday morning as I was : making breakfast, checking email, trying to finish some planning and I'm sure something else - probably checking Facebook or something else completely useless. (And so you know, I just detoured from writing this (BE) to text my boss (about) something that happened this a.m. at the gym. I am hopeless!!!!)

Anyway, I sort of percolated over the whole be single minded in my actions and focus when I am doing a task this week and sometimes I was able to do it and sometimes not.

I also realize that the reason I need so many goll-darn lists everywhere is because I AM such a scatter brain. My brain is constantly in action, turned on, thinking, creating, moving through the slide show that is my day. I hope that maybe you can understand this mind-switching game. It's actually a little torturous at times as it makes it difficult to get all of those darn lists DONE. I do have bright moments though when I will just see something and attack it and see it through then move onto the next thing.

So my practice is to incorporate more and more the ability to focus on a single, solitary task - or person or thought or intention - when it is truly in my best interest. There are times when doing automatic things along with thinking things is fine. So I will cut myself a little slack on that. We can't "BE...focused" 100% of the time. If I were absolutely perfect at all of your "BE's" life would BEcome very boring!!! Oh, I'm so glad I can make myself laugh. NOW. Off to do some errands, each of which I will complete in full before beginning the next. AND I will NOT NOT NOT make lists as I go..............hmmm so I better make those lists now I guess. Just to be safe and all. Wouldn't want to miss out on an opportunity to think about 10 things at once or to do 5 or 6 if they are on the list.

Oh 1 more thing about when it's ok to not focus on 1 thing....carrying groceries, mail, and anything else up from the garage to the house. I am all about the fewest trips with the most stuff. I think it's completely acceptable to put as many of those tasks together as possible. AND to pick up anything along the way that happens to arise - laundry down, shoes up, things put away along the way.......

Love, Multi-tasking Maven Marny

And next week our FOCUS will be on .....BE...supportive. Great, I get to be a human BRA! hahaha

SUPPORTIVE

From: **Marny Jaastad** (marnymarie@yahoo.com)

To: evanmccleerybrown@yahoo.com

Date: Saturday, August 17, 2013 6:11 AM

Evan!

I actually feel really great about this week's word. At first I was a little skeptical and maybe even a little "ho-hum" about it. BE...supportive? I mean really, that's basically the definition of my job! But I discovered many ways in which I could do that. And I also discovered that looking at the word every morning, or whenever I'm at my desk, really does infuse it into my subconscious......as you can see when you read below......

My goal this week is (was) to identify and target ONE PERSON each day who could use a little support.....a shoulder, an ear, a leg up, a boost, a kiss, a hug, whatever! And my hope in being supportive is to pay it forward. We all need someone/something sometime so mine will come back around to meet me when I need it. (So these are in reverse order obviously, but it's sort of interesting to read them that way as well......)

Day 5... a little lower key day. Today I took my task literally because I have an older client - Burt Bacharach - who you won't know as famous but he is really, really famous AND really, really OLD! He trains with me in the summers - he likes to go to the beach and the racetrack! - and for 85, he is quite fit. But he's had 2 shoulder replacements so I actually have to HOLD his shoulder in place while he does some exercises. I am literally his support system! Haha.   My brain must be in "support" mode because I also decided to make my "Monday Challenge" - which I put up on my Facebook page every Monday - about BEing...supportive. I am challenging everyone to go to a website I know which rates charities, choose one that resonates with them, "LIKE" it and therefore, *support* it! My hope is that they will truly discover a charity to support and that others who read their FB pages will as well. Kind of a viral awareness campaign for charities in general. You can check out some that you might want to support - with your voice if not with $$$ - at http://www.charitynavigator.org. There might even be one to support something about baseball! hahaha

Day 4......holy moly makin' up for Day 3. Everyone needed something today. I think the one that stands out the most - and to whom I really gave all of my energy was my last client. She was literally having an anxiety attack as she came into train. Worried about 3 boys, brother, work, life in general and couldn't catch her breath. She looked at me with on-the-verge-of-tears eyes and said "I feel like my chest is being crushed." I set her down on a bench, took her hands in mine, had her shut her eyes and then practice yoga breathing. B-I-G inhale through the nose, hold it, sip a little more air, hold it and release through the mouth like a soft "ha"......we did it 3 times and I could feel the energy leaving my hands and going into her body but I could also WATCH her relaxing. Wow, sometimes our brains can spin us to places that we need to have someone come rescue us from. I felt very good about BEing....supportive.

Day 3......Hmmmmm nothing standing out especially to me. I have tried to not *actively* seek out someone to "support" but rather to be struck when it does occur. Today I really decided to support ME. I had the opportunity to have a little break when someone cancelled and I took it! Normally I would contact a few other clients to let them know that I could see them that day, even on short notice. But I decided to get myself caught up on things "on my list." Getting my head cleared makes it easier to be a supportive person and friend to others because I am less focused internally and more perceptive externally. Being supportive I find is most definitely about being externally aware of what is going on around you and within others.

Day2.....I was running down a pretty busy street and a soccer ball came rolling out - with the proverbial "small child following it". I put my hand out toward the child and stopped him - he was LITTLE!!! - and there was a car coming too. It all happened so quickly I didn't even think. I kicked the ball back while I was running and told him he was *very good* to stop and to never, never, never follow the ball. It's not quite the "supportive" that I thought I would BE this week but I am pretty sure it counts in the realm of supporting life!

Day 1 - one of my client's grand-daughters is going to college on Thursday and is pretty nervous. She (grand-daughter) lost her mom just 1 year ago and has not really been able to cope with that very well. So I made her a card wishing her luck and telling her she can contact me anytime she needs: to talk, yell, celebrate, laugh, whatever......

Everyone needs a lift and a little extra help now and then. You'll be surprised how even this smallest gesture of BEing...supportive can impact someone's life....

Love you tons (and I ALWAYS support you!),
Marny

Next up............BE...encouraged! Oooh FUN. I like optimism.

ENCOURAGED

Subject: Be...encouraged

From: **Marny Jaastad** (marnymarie@yahoo.com)

To: evanmccleerybrown@yahoo.com

Date: Monday, August 26, 2013 2:39 PM

Hi Evan!

My very first thought was, "Hmmm, BE...encouragED not encouragING?" Hmmm. So that to me means being more RECEPTIVE to what is coming at me in terms of motivation versus being the motivator! Let's see where we go with it this week.

I am encouraged today (Sunday 8.18.13) by my OWN performance in my last 1/2 marathon for 2013. I have now completed 21 of them....cannot believe that sometimes. I had really fallen into quite a blasé rut with running and pretty much just pounded out the miles to get them over with. So I made a deal with myself that today I would run to: feel good, not kill myself, not be in the wrong kind of pain, be proud of simply finishing. And I accomplished all of that. So I am re-energized and ENCOURAGED about my running again...............after I take some time off though!

I am also (re-)encouraged to continue my quest for "living my dreams" and in looking at what it will take to bring me to that point. Or at least closer and closer each day. New job opportunities, new relationships with people who are more like "me", new hobbies??? Who knows......going to let things show up and see if they interest me. I have to also say that this has been my only spot of "dis"couragement this week. I had been applying for a job that you have to take a very difficult 3 hour online test for. And after 2 tries I still had not achieved the level I had to for their requirements. So I was pretty down on myself but as I paid a little more attention to how I felt, I realized that I was also *relieved*. This position would have been all on my own time, but it would have added 20 hours per week to my already pretty packed schedule. So in the end I am ENCOURAGED to look elsewhere if I want to try a new job! I guess I can't deny that something out there is sending me a pretty strong message, ENCOURAGING me, to make another choice. But who doesn't like to succeed, right??

As I continued to ponder and explore exactly what I thought this BE might mean for me I finally got "IT" - for me that is. First: BE...encouraged, as in RECEIVE encouragement, take it in from others, the world, the universe, where ever. I am so used to BEing encouragING - the giver, the doer, the active versus passive participant. Once I re-framed my view I started seeing all means of receiving encouragement.....

And as I am so wont to do, I like to pull apart complex words like this one. BE...EN-COURAGE-D. Courage stood out like a beacon flagging me down. COURAGE: be not afraid, have strength in the face of adversity or uncertainty; move forward into what may be complete darkness. When I saw this little gem how could I not think of the Cowardly Lion from the Wizard of Oz?? He sought courage from the Wizard and trusted his friends and in the end, himself, really, to just move forward, no matter what presented itself. Dorothy and the Tin Man provided no end of encouragement where he thought he had none.

So here I find myself hand-in-hand with the Cowardly Lion, headed toward Oz down the Yellow Brick Road.......oh what might bring itself my way if I am only to BE...ENCOURAGED by what may fall out of the forest or the poppy field or the witch's castle as I make my journey.....
lots of xo's

I hope that you will also BE...encouraged by your new school and new year and new opportunities. I am always right here to offer any courage, strength and certainty that you need.
Marny

And our next investigation to BE...on time! Oh this one MUST be for YOU! haha - be on time to school!

ON TIME

Be...on time

From: **Marny Jaastad** (marnymarie@yahoo.com)

To: evanmccleerybrown@yahoo.com

Date: Monday, September 2, 2013 4:05 PM

Dear Evan

Happy Day Off of School! (which I hope you are loving! New school, people, classes, etc...... can't wait for stories but I digress from the point at hand...)

Every clock I own is set a minimum of 5 minutes ahead. If I am on time, I am late by my book!

What I find this to mean for me is to BE...on time - as in in-synch with what is going on around me. Having good timing in how I deal with people and situations and life. I have learned over time that I have to think just a few seconds longer than I might otherwise before opening my mouth and spilling forth with what is in my head. Because what is really clear to me is that timing is EVERYTHING. I have learned to gauge people's temperament and mood as to their receptiveness to what I want to convey. The same statement, meaning and delivery can be received completely differently depending upon my being ON TIME with my approach.

The above really applies to me personally to BE...on time. But I also like to look at the meaning and direction that these phrases can mean for people in general. When I apply them to myself, I tend to look deeper into the meaning and find a more symbolic intention. As I worked this one over in my head more this week, I thought for everyone in general what does it *literally* mean to be on time. What are the implications of literally arriving where you are supposed to be, doing what you are supposed to do, etc. at/by the specified time? And I concluded that to BE...on time is to indicate one's lack of selfishness. It is to state, tacitly, that "I am not more important than you. Your time, work, effort, your actual being does not take a backseat to me and my time, work, effort and being." That said, the importance tied to BE...on time becomes even greater - and I have observed more and more these days that it has also become less common. Excuses abound as to why someone is late. And if you listen well, the reasons for being tardy all fall on others' shoulders. That slow person driving in front of me. That slow checker at the grocery store. My slow kids......

Finally, I thought about the bigger picture of 1 person being late. Sort of along the lines of a ripple in a pond from a dropped stone - growing out, out, out toward the edges of the pond. The ripple of 1 person being late reverberates forward. A doctor has to then push all of their patients to later. Everyone gets thrown off. OR the doctor makes YOU late and then YOUR day gets thrown off to others. You come late to a class and interrupt everyone and then they have to make room for you and you have to "catch up" to where everyone already is in class. People rarely consider the ramifications or future consequences of their one infraction to NOT BE...on time. Like the proverbial Butterfly Effect - when a small event, like the beating wings of a butterfly - may alter the course of weather to say change the path of a tornado. Yes, a little dramatic I agree, but you get the point.

SO where are we? I think that to BE...on time is to demonstrate the greatest humility one can towards another. It is an act beyond respect but of validation of another's worth and the esteem that you hold for them.
In the end really all I mean is don't miss the bus to school. Yah, I know (you) don't ride the bus. You know what I mean!

Lots of Labor Day Love,
Marny

DISCIPLINED

Hi Evan

First week of school down and conquered. Hardest part over; now it's just homework and steady focus.....so how perfect that this week was BE...disciplined??!?

Ooooooh. That's good stuff. Now I could take the snarky approach as I did with be ...encouraged and say that this must mean that I am to TAKE discipline. As in be disciplined by someone but I think I will forgo that route and take it at face value. (To mean) the act of having discipline.
I always like to check out synonyms of my BE words....some good ones to play with here: addicted, confirmed, trained, in the habit......I like them all for different reasons.

I find discipline to be the fine line or tight rope between apathy and obsession. We like to think that discipline is a highly esteemed trait to possess. HOWEVER when discipline falls over the edge to obsession and interferes with one's day to day life, it can be dangerous. By the same token, the slippery slope theory goes that if we lose our discipline - less time practicing, studying, being a good person - the more we fall into apathy and take on bad characteristics. So how do we find the happy, middle, safe ground? I think that there are several ways that we evaluate having good discipline: our own assessments; friends, family and outsiders who know us; and even strangers. Ourselves: we can turn a mirror upon ourselves and ask "Am I sticking to the task at hand? Am I devoting too much time and effort to one part of my life only? Am I then ignoring other parts of my life which deserve equal attention and devotion?"

Friends/Family: They observe and make comments, or not, judgments, or not, and provide perspective which we simply cannot possess about ourselves no matter the extent to which we can TRY to be objective. "Should you be spending more time on your homework and less time practicing pitching?"

"Should you be getting outside and letting your mind and body relax and recover rather than do 10 more math problems?"
Strangers: "Do you always spend so much time doing that one task?"

Discipline = balance. I never thought of it that way. I am always told by people, "You are so *focused*. You concentrate so well. Your DISCIPLINE is unbelievable......" And I have always taken those to be positive comments about which I can be proud. But this week, I looked from the outside in. I asked myself - mostly when I was going to do a workout or add "just one" more client to my schedule, "Is this discipline or is this over the edge? What am I sacrificing to be "disciplined" about making money or staying healthy? Good questions.

My drive to be disciplined stems from the desire to (be) viewed as virtuous, good and admirable. I want people to respect me. Who doesn't, right?!? Haha. But it CAN go too far. I know Santa won't bring me any extra presents because I am disciplined. Haha again. But you know what I mean. I think that good things will come to me if I sacrifice and go without and work hard and even deprive myself a little. Not so! I only end up miserable and tired and not rewarded. I have vowed to find my rewards FROM my discipline not as a result of the discipline itself.......a pretty lofty goal but I've got plenty of help along the way. Walking the tightrope could be a good mental exercise for me....as long as I don't practice TOO MUCH!

xoxox
Marny

Hope you are loving your new school and activities and life.....and that you too can BE...disciplined in a successful way!

INQUISITIVE

Subject:	Be...inquisitive! AKA WHAT IF!?!?!?
From:	**Marny Jaastad** (marnymarie@yahoo.com)
To:	evanmccleerybrown@yahoo.com
Date:	Sunday, September 15, 2013 5:29 PM

Hi Evan

I actually wondered all week - inquisitively!! - how you have been doing in school. I really do hope that you are liking it, meeting some cool peeps and maybe even liking some of your classes!

Oh am I ever gonna have fun with THIS! I am going to drive people, animals, inanimate objects and the world in general crazy asking questions and checking things out! Hmmmmm, what does THIS button do?!?!? hahahaha
I challenge you to see how inquisitive YOU can be at school, soccer, home.......(ok, but don't get in trouble trying to see if Jaden's head fits in the toilet! It DOES NOT!)

In retrospect I realize that I employed my inquisitive powers this week by pushing boundaries. By that I mean I asked a lot of "what if....?" questions. For instance, I saw an opportunity for a new area to study in training and a potential new program to try to make money. But I didn't know where I might offer it. Since it is something that I would develop, I didn't really think my boss would see it as an opportunity for the gym.....but you never know til you ask, right??? So I did (ask) and he is interested. We'll see how THAT develops.
Then, I got invited to a party - no biggie, right? Except that it was on a work night and later than I would normally be up to go to work the next day. But I asked myself - what's the worst that could happen? I'll be tired! The opportunity to meet some new people, maybe make some new friends, and try a new restaurant out-weighed losing a little sleep. And because I asked "what if?" I found: some new friends, a great new restaurant AND I wasn't tired....
Then a place that I take a class at every week emailed everyone and said, "We are closing in 2 weeks. Sorry." End of story. WHOA!! But I had paid for more classes than I would be able to take before they closed. I had resigned myself to the fact that I would lose that money since they said that there wouldn't be

104

refunds. BUT then I thought, NOPE. I am not satisfied with that. So I asked if I could use the remainder of the money from my sessions to buy something from their store. And.....the manager said YES! WOW! All I had to do was ask.

These may seem to be silly examples of BE...inquisitive BUT what they demonstrate is that just because something is done a certain way, or your daily routine is a certain way or you put your shoes on the same way every day does NOT mean that it must remain so. How would the world ever change if no one ever asked "what if?" If no one dared to wonder, and test out, what might happen if something were done a different way, in a different order, on a different planet......yes, really. Even now we are talking about people going to Mars and trying to live on the journey there and possibly back. Or colonizing the moon, or just simply putting your left shoe on before your right.

So never be afraid to ask the simple or the complex questions when they strike you. When something catches your eye and you *wonder* what it (might) do or be or become, try to find out. Ask questions, seek answers, do not be satisfied with "because I said so...." BE...inquisitive. You never know, you might just end up flying to Mars.....

Love you very much and I wonder just where you *will* end up some day, doing what, being the best you that can, as I know you will.
Marny

Are you ready to BE...OBSERVANT??? Because that's next. What a GREAT follow up to be inquisitive. After asking "what if" we can then begin to OBSERVE what happens WHEN! Stay tuned, I'll get my microscope out for the week.

OBSERVANT

Be...observant

From: **Marny Jaastad** (marnymarie@yahoo.com)

To: evanmccleerybrown@yahoo.com

Date: Sunday, September 22, 2013 6:37 PM

Helllooooo Evan!

Listen, look, feel, touch, smell...that pretty much sums up BE...observant for me. The Five Senses. Our tools for BEing observant of our world, others, life, the mind......WAIT! The mind??? Smell, touch, taste, feel, listen.....hmmmm maybe not so much. BE...observant may be more complex than I thought.

It is easy to observe OUTside of oneself - other people, a bug, a group of people at a park.....but to turn one's observations to ONESELF and notice how our behavior, attitude and demeanor affect others is a whole 'nother ball of wax, as they say. I am challenging myself to see and to listen to myself when it comes to my effect on others. We communicate so much with non-verbal cues: crossed arms, "faces" (raised eyebrows, frowns, SMILES!, rolled eyes....). What I observed the other day was HOW MUCH I and really all of us use these cues to subconsciously say a whole lot to other people. I had a conversation with a friend about the faces that we make and how transparent that makes us to others (when we might actually think we are holding back reactions/comments).

So I decided to BE...observant about MY effect on others' behavior purely from the standpoint of non-verbal cues. Interesting experiment. Obviously being aware of the fact that I was watching myself caused me to hold back slightly on my facial and body language expressions BUT it was interesting. Because we get so used to ourselves, we don't "observe" ourselves the way we "observe" others (well mostly, since some of my clients tune me out or check out in general in the gym!). It was interesting for me to catch myself in the myriad mirrors we have in the gym and see the expressions that I didn't even realize I was making! OOOPS - did anyone see that? And here's what I observed: the more I tried NOT to make faces, the more I said things under my breath. Oh, well THAT is not a good alternative. So maybe I will stick with the faces and body language instead of the actual words. Safer since I never know who might overhear me. But in all seriousness, I really tried to BE...observant of *why* those facial expressions or inadvertent mutterings came out. It seems to be human nature to need to really watch each other when we speak or interact even non-verbally. To *observe* every aspect of communication. I did also notice that we humans really do *observe* and pick apart or analyze or talk about what we watch others do and say.

There is, of course, an entire other direction and meaning to take and to BE...observant about. It is wholly religious, and I feel, just as important as the more common definition related to being aware or tuned into some specific act or event. I guess the religious sense of the word does also relate to awareness and being focused on a specific teaching or sacred day or a religious practice in general. "Are you observant?" people will ask around various holiday times. It having just been Yom Kippur, this alternate way of thinking about BE...observant came to my mind more readily than it might have. In Judaism this is the day of atonement and reflection and for establishing your goals for the new year. The Jewish calendar is lunar based and so does not match up with the calendar we use in everyday life. It brought me to wonder if you are still attending church and continuing to enjoy that as well? And I wondered if you might consider yourself to BE...observant of a particular religion? Or maybe you just enjoy the company of others you have met there and are learning some interesting history and teachings.

In whatever way we choose to BE...observant, it is an important part of evaluating ourselves, others, the world around us, life in general. Closing off and shutting down from input that is constantly coming our way is like sitting in a windowless, door-less, dark room: empty. Observing provides us the opportunity to enrich ourselves and our lives.

I hope you observe many interesting and useful - or even not useful, maybe just entertaining - things this week.
Love you muchly
Marny

Here we go with BE...PREPARED! I *love* it! Just like the Boy Scouts! (ok, maybe girl scouts in my case.....) I'm already 1/2 way there because I am READY to take this one on!

PREPARED

From: **Marny Jaastad** (marnymarie@yahoo.com)

To: evanmccleerybrown@yahoo.com

Date: Monday, September 30, 2013 5:58 PM

Hello Hello Evan!

Well I think you guys are in the middle of some serious wetness right now. Oh boy, fall and winter in Seattle......such a good time. Well then it is so appropriate that this week we got to BE...prepared! So I hope you have: umbrella, HIGH boots, rain jacket and maybe even a snorkel. Yeah, I know, not funny, Marny. Ok, well maybe a little.....

Boy Scouts aside, being prepared is very important to me. As I thought about *why* that is so I recognized that it provides me with a feeling of safety and certainty. I like to know what is ahead and that I am ready for whatever that may be. I am not so good at surprises or at managing curve balls that get thrown my way. Wish I could say that I am a fly-by-the-seat-of-your-pants kinda gal, but NOPE. Not for me.

However as I began to think more about how to BE....prepared, I came back to the Boy Scouts. In that sense, they are told to BE...prepared for some *unknown*. "If you have all of these skills that we teach you, you will be able to live in the woods all alone and survive, no matter what comes your way." They will BE...prepared! However, there is no certainty that they will meet up with any situation that may make their being prepared useful. So I believe one can BE...prepared for the "just in case" situations in life. As I said, for me, to BE...prepared is for the "absolutely going to happen" situations in life. I would argue that the "just in case" scenarios of the absolutely going to happen cases are really *contingency plans*. For which one may - or may not- be specifically prepared.

So this tiny little life we lead on this big old Earth is really a series of WHAT IF's isn't it? I mean what to BE...prepared for if not the WHAT IF's that present themselves. WHAT IF I win the lottery? WHAT IF some man sweeps me off my feet and takes me to Alaska? WHAT IF I wake up bald? (Pretty much rules out some man sweeping me off my feet, huh?) You get the point. By nature we

110

wonder about the unknown. The WHAT IF....? So we continually must
BE...prepared for the THEN. BE...prepared is the "THEN" for WHAT IF?

As I do with so many of these words, I looked it up! Both for the meanings given
as well as its origin since BE..."pared" is not a use that "pre-" would follow
logically......here's what I found:

: made at an earlier time for later use : made ready in advance

: ready for something : in a suitable condition for some purpose or activity

: willing *to do* something

Yah, I buy all of those. Those all mean BE...prepared.

Maybe in the end the Boy Scouts should say BE... well-learned in the skills of
survival! hahaha Since I think that to BE...prepared indicates a readiness for a
specific situation, action or event. For the WHAT IF's of life.....

Lots of love. And BE...prepared for the weather to come. At least you
can *kinda* guess what it will be like and hedge your bets.

Marny

Drum roll please.....next week we are off to the exploration of how to
BE...humble. Guess I can't tell you about how great I am at BE...humble can I?
I guess I will be successful with an aw shucks, it was nuthin' at the end of the
week (even though I know I'm a rock star) hee hee

HUMBLE

Subject: **Be...humble**

From: **Marny Jaastad** (marnymarie@yahoo.com)

To: evanmccleerybrown@yahoo.com

Date: Sunday, October 6, 2013 4:34 PM

Hi Ev

So this actually got harder and harder the most I thought about it. Actually it got more depressing in a way because I realized that our current society is SOOOO self-focused and so supportive of self-declaration and proclamation of greatness that we might not ever get back to a time when people know how to be humble. In a time when everyone and anyone can tell you what an amazing salad they just made - complete with pictures and recipe - via FaceBook, Instagram or Twitter. How will we ever re-teach each other to be humble to NOT tout our (not so) impressive accomplishments? I don't have the answer to that BUT I do know what I think about BE...humble and how I plan to approach our self-absorbed society!

Wow. This will be interesting. How to proclaim one's success at being humble. Guess it will have to be very, very subtle and understated.

BE... humble. I have spent quite a bit of time just purely pondering this one. Often I will write throughout the week as to my thoughts and awakenings on each of these BE's. However, this one has had me just.....thinkin'. I have realized that I often remind myself that I need to BE...humble. However, maybe not so directly or specifically as this. I have a little note on my clipboard at work "get off the horse." As in, "get off your high horse, because you are not so good as you think you are." In life there will always be someone "better" - whatever that might mean. There could be an actual, demonstrable, measurable better - faster in the 50 yd dash; able to hit or throw farther in baseball; higher grade point average in school. All of those are clear when it comes to "better" and being humble about one's own status. BUT, there is also always going to be someone you will be better THAN. And since it will be obvious to both of you, why would you take the energy and exhibit the arrogance to make a point of it? (Neither) You nor I - nor anyone - would. At least we would hope so. I have actually found this to NOT always be the case. One of the greatest things I was ever taught in rowing and competition was that you *never* make anyone feel badly for the effort that they have put forth. Always compliment, thank, acknowledge that someone has worked/tried/given it their all. TODAY you may be better, but tomorrow is another opportunity and another chance for someone else to be better. So BE...humble in your achievements.

Now, as to being humble in a more general sense. To be humble in life when there is no concrete measure of better. That is a much more difficult challenge - even to identify how/when one might need to be aware of it. Humility is a virtue that I believe actually puts you "ABOVE" another individual. It demonstrates more fully the ability to achieve and need no self-recognition for it.

In addition, allowing your focus to drift away from you and your accomplishments provides the opportunity to learn from and to see the value and worth in others. What could we see and learn from another if we are to simply accept that we have faults and that we are not perfect? Our society is so focused on achievement at all costs and on individual recognition, that learning how to utilize the knowledge, skills and achievements of OTHERS for our benefit is clouded over and elusive.

Now of course the final challenge is how to BE...humble without seeming as though you are fishing for compliments! Again that "fine line" that always seems to exist in life. So many times people are self-deprecating. "Oh, that wasn't that good." "Oh I don't cook (play baseball, paint) that well." You know the types. What they are really saying is "Tell me how awesome I am!" Being truly humble then is an art in and of itself. It is the sense of an actual belief that there are others better than you. That you do have faults. That you can always be taught and can learn from others. This is the admired, esteemed and respected individual. And likely the one who is actually "the better", "the faster", the "more" of whatever is in question.....

Good luck in all that you do, always. But remember, keep yourself in check...BE...humble.
love, Marny

We're off to the land of BE...in nature. Ok! Sounds good to me! Wanna come down here and go play in the ocean???

IN NATURE

From: **Marny Jaastad** (marnymarie@yahoo.com)

To: evanmccleerybrown@yahoo.com

Date: Friday, October 11, 2013 6:30 PM

Happy Friday evening Evan,

BE...in nature.....and why might that be so important to have made the list of The 72 BE's??? Welllllll let's investigate why.

I am going to be VERY successful at this one.

I may have to do a daily update.

First, a little literature review, as always.....

"Being outside in nature makes people feel more alive, finds a series of studies published in the June 2010 issue of the *Journal of Environmental Psychology*. And that sense of increased vitality exists above and beyond the energizing effects of physical activity and social interaction that are often associated with our forays into the natural world."
"Nature is fuel for the soul"

And there you have it, from SCIENCE!
I especially like the part about fuel for the SOUL. That would pretty much sum up what I discovered in my little BE...in nature experiment.

Today, Sunday, I ran OUTSIDE in the beautiful a.m. cool, crisp, with a hint of the Santa Ana wind and HEAT that came later. Then later I took myself for a walk around the block. Small, yes, but significant. Why is it that nature draws us in?

Monday, I took a nice brisk power walk to run errands rather than drive - done specifically because of my BE this week. And I wanted to truly notice how I felt doing so. It was just so nice to be outside! DUH! I felt much less time pressure - though it was a Monday no different than any other and I still had the same things to get done. I began to think that it is THE SUN, our big old star up there, which is what really draws us to BE ...in nature. But I am not so sure of that since sometimes it's nice as well to let the rain fall on your face. Though maybe not in Seattle where that is status quo for the majority of the year.

Not out and about a lot today BUT the interesting thing is that it was cloudy and I was most definitely LESS drawn to BE...in nature than when the sun was out yesterday and previous days. Interesting. This furthers my belief that it is not nature per se, but THE SUN that beckons us out!! And I remembered when I was coaching many years ago that I spent so much time OUT that I actually truly reveled in being INside at times. Grass is always greener as they say.

And we (here in San Diego) were ALL IN NATURE last night. WHEW! Great thunderstorm - which we never, ever get. It is always fascinating for me to observe animal's behavior in "weather" and climatic events. Animals know well before we do that something is coming. It is yet one more indication that we should all BE... in nature as often as we can. Maybe it goes back to the good old caveman days. Living outside was the only choice. It's nice to have shelter and all but look at all the camping that people do now, all over the world.

The thing I realize when I am "in nature" is that I *notice* a lot more going on. Since I am not trapped in a vehicle, I hear, see, feel things that I would otherwise miss. And I am always curious when I am outside in the city what others are doing out walking at that time as well. Encountering people when out hiking or in a park or the woods, it's pretty darn obvious what they are out for. But do others choose to walk to the grocery store as I do because it's nice to be OUT or do they not have that choice? Yesterday's Grocery Walk actually became a little bit of an inside joke to myself as I spent nearly the entire walk back (home) TEXTING! Well gee that sure ruins the goal of BE... in nature. I laughed when I realized I was home already and had missed most of my "BE" experience. Still.....the sun, the breeze, the air was nice.......I felt more able to tackle the remainder of my day - and more enthusiastic about doing so as well after being in nature.

I see Mom this weekend in LA. Definitely not going to BE...in nature there! Hotel, concert, hotel, maybe outside walking around but in downtown LA, the only nature is the oddity of the people wandering around.

I liked BE... in nature. It was a great reminder more than anything of the need to refuel my soul every day - several times a day - and get OUT.
Hope you are able to re-fuel as well this weekend and BE...in nature.

Mom and I will update you on the nature we encounter at the concert! hahaha
Love, Marny

Are you ready to BE...adventurous? Cause I sure am! And HOW FUNNY. I just texted Mom that this weekend was going to be an adventure! I must be prescient! But I guess we knew that.....Psychic Godmother and all. (Evan gave me a charm bracelet and one charm read "psychic godmother")

ADVENTUROUS

Be...adventurous

From: **Marny Jaastad** (marnymarie@yahoo.com)

To: evanmccleerybrown@yahoo.com

Date: Tuesday, October 22, 2013 5:39 PM

Dear Evan -

I love this.......chose it the night before I was leaving to meet Mom for the P!NK concert in LA. Talk about being adventurous. This is so out of my usual very, very routine life. All about adventure. Haven't even planned a thing beyond driving directions! Wow, what a crazy lady, I know. hahahahaha

It was quite the adventure. And as adventure is supposed to yield, was a good way to "shake things up." We of course have to look at the definition of adventure for each person because for the majority of the world, my "adventure" to P!NK and LA was run-of-the-mill life as usual. Nothing that would shake up their world. I was also reminded of a quote that often comes to my mind when I feel like my life has become a little stale. "Life is either a daring adventure or nothing at all." I'm not sure it's quite that cut and dried.....but adventure certainly has its place in life! Now what is really amazing about that quote.........It's from HELEN KELLER!!! Of all people. Certainly not someone we might think of as possibly even being capable of being adventurous in the way that it is traditionally seen. Every step she took may have been an adventure for her. She also said that "Security is mostly a superstition." Well there you have it. Even when we "play it safe", there is no guarantee of security. So with that in mind..........let's take the leap of faith and BE...adventurous!!!!!!!

But adventure intones some amount of risk or hazard, something requiring courage to undertake. So maybe I didn't have a "real" adventure. The only risk came when I lost the sole of my shoe crossing the street! That was definitely one for the books.

So why is being adventurous good for us? Why would we strive to be adventurous? I am not sure. Is there a calculation that we make about a potential adventure that says: "Well the risks and hazards associated with the potential AWESOME outcome of X do not outweigh the possibility that the outcome will be achieved." At what point is adventure purely folly and a dangerous or at the least un-wise undertaking? Maybe (that point is) at the risk of life and limb, as they say. Or is *mental* injury and risk as important a factor in assessing whether to set out on an adventure?

Over my life I certainly have pursued other great adventures. I hiked for a month on the Appalachian Trail, I bought and renovated a nearly 100 year old house - from mostly all the way down to the studs - I set out to make (and did) the US National Rowing Team. All have been adventures. All have had some amount of risk and or hazard associated with them. Physical, financial, mental and spiritual.

It is interesting that BE...adventurous almost always connotes some sort of outside, risky trip or expedition taking place in the nether-regions of the world. "Adventurers" are people like Sir Edmund Hillary, Amundson, Columbus.....all were noted for their feats in "taking on" nature. Maybe not taming it per se but certainly going to see what they could see. Similar to but also quite different from BE...in nature, their drive was most definitely not for rejuvenation and to feel better, as we saw with last week's BE but with curiosity, challenge and maybe a little wanderlust. I think today we would call them adrenaline junkies. Taking that leap of faith. There is that little bit of a rush and excitement you get from not knowing exactly how something might turn out when you step out into an adventure - whether in your backyard or the uncharted regions of some desolate landscape.

Would we consider astronauts to BE...adventurous? Or is that a terrestrial term? Is flying to the moon - and back - "just their job"? Or maybe this is the ultimate adventure. I think a mission trumps an adventure any day. It seems adventure intones some level of free will and very little planning; to the extent that space travel would entail (planning) at least.

In the end I think I will adopt the tenor of Ms. Keller. Security is an illusion. Adventure is that which takes you past your comfort zone - be that your front door or the frozen arctic tundra. Adventure is in our HEART, in our imagination, in our approach to the world. We are all explorers of the greatest degree.

Have a very adventurous week. Hope you find something never before known - well at least by you - but maybe by mankind!

xoxox always
Marny

I'm all worn out after my adventures so I am glad that now I get to BE...spirited and soulful. Wow...I am not even sure how one does that. And THAT, my dear Evan, is the whole point of BE...ing!!!!!

SPIRITED & SOULFUL

Subject:	Be...spirited and soulful
From:	**Marny Jaastad** (marnymarie@yahoo.com)
To:	evanmccleerybrown@yahoo.com
Date:	Sunday, October 27, 2013 4:31 PM

Hi Evan

So this one kind of caught me by surprise in the amount that it really brought up a lot of emotions and senses and memories. There is a heck of a lot going on with this BE and it took a lot of energy when I really set my mind to it. This is one of the ones that will kind of "go in the box". By that I mean it will come up again and again for me. The importance of equal and opposite, of point and counterpoint.

At first glance those may seem very unrelated BE's.....however, as usual I am determined (and fully capable) of finding their connection and similarity. Their sameness and their interwoven qualities.

I believe that this is the Western equivalent to Yin and Yang. The equal and opposite yet uniting properties of the world as seen in Chinese philosophy. One cannot know light without dark, happiness without sadness, nor how to BE...soulful if one is not able to BE...spirited.

Being soulful last night as I watched a piece on the news about some middle school football players and an amazing act of kindness that they did for a fellow teammate. A little cry does the heart good sometimes. Just a small tear down the cheek, but it reminds one of the depth and purity of simple emotion.

And to follow that up with being spirited! I had taken a donation-based yoga class yesterday to support a huge bike ride this weekend for cancer - Pedal The Cause - which was a ride out to Julian and back - 1 day each way. WHEW! Quite a big deal. Well today as I was out walking I saw one of the aid stations with 3 people there. I asked them if there were still people coming through and they said the LAST FOUR were just about to come around the corner!!! So as they came by, I, all by my little lonesome, started clapping and cheering and jumping up and down for them. I was so proud to have been part of something so amazing and to have given my strength in class to these people and my donation outside of class to help with finding a cure for cancer. And concomitant with that - moving to the soulful side - I began to think of all of the people, families, groups I know who have been touched by cancer. Those who are survivors, have passed, are in the throes of their battle and I was sad and somber. I continued on my walk sending my thoughts to all of those people and their families - even mine.

The above are merely specific examples of the soulful and spirited week that I had. I am sure as you look back you can see similar experiences in your week and your life. As I walked today it really hit me even more deeply that when I think about how to BE...spirited, I envision a little elfin creature or a pixie prancing about and having boundless energy, a lightness, an almost levitating quality about it. And when I think of how to BE...soulful, I immediately see some old, grizzled, bent over blues or jazz singer, crooning on about a tough life and lost love and wholly putting the pain and emotional depth of life right out there for all to share and to bear.

I came to realize that the two states of being are really quite related to youth (pixie, elf, sprite) and age (wisdom, experience, reflection). This is not to say in any way you too cannot be soulful, being that you are certainly not OLD and that I cannot be spirited, though I may have lost some of my abilities to levitate! As we move through life, we are afforded the opportunity to experience both of them. Sometimes simultaneously and sometimes at vastly different points in our lives.

In either case, let them each fall upon you and welcome them. They are each so important for our experience of the world and of who we are.

Lots of very spirited love cradled with deep soulful reflection on the amazing times we have spent together.
Marny

Wow.....heavy stuff. Maybe next week will lighten me up a bit as I attempt to BE...respectful. Oh absolutely. This is definitely going to be all about the practice I think. And maybe less so about the philosophy and deeper meaning of it.

RESPECTFUL

Subject: Be...respectful

From: **Marny Jaastad** (marnymarie@yahoo.com)

To: evanmccleerybrown@yahoo.com

Date: Sunday, November 3, 2013 4:08 PM

My Dear Sir, Evan McCleery Brown:......(being respectful and all)

Always. If there is a quality or descriptor that I can say I would want anyone to say about me, it is that I am RESPECTFUL.

I have walked/run/yoga-ed, and just generally sat and truly chewed away on just what it means - in the pith of it - to BE...respectful. And yes, it means saying thank you and please and not stepping in front of someone and taking off your hat for the national anthem and those such things. But WHAT at its heart does it mean to BE...respectful.

And boy do I hate to pull the age card out on this one...............BUT because I AM old(er) and I have been able to look back over a (whole) lot of years, what I finally concluded is that one must look beyond the end of one's own nose. And by that I mean.......

"Kids these days...." you will often hear people say about behavior/music/choice of dress/RESPECT. But I firmly believe and will put forth with *evidence* that ADULTS these days as well have become so self-absorbed, narcissistic and egocentric that it has become impossible for anyone to be respectful to anyone else. They can't get out of their own way long enough to focus any attention ON someone else. Ok, so I am being quite harsh here and I am definitely exaggerating.......but not by a lot! A simple search on Wikipedia of "major active social networking sites" (which does NOT include dating websites) around the world, came up with 201!!!!!! sites. And these are
"limited to notable, well-known sites" according to Wiki. HOLY COW! No wonder no one has time to pay respect to someone else. They have 201 sites that they have to prove their awesomeness and wonderfulness on! Ok, enough with being snarky and snide. I'm as guilty as, well maybe only 5%, of the country. I "do" FB and LinkedIn and that's about it. I don't have a smartphone; it (my phone) is quite dumb actually. And I am pretty proud of that fact. I like that I can't take a "selfie" and right away post it to FB or some other site. I'd rather take note of what's going on around me and pay attention to the person I

127

am with than to be concerned and obsessed with me.

Before: FB, Instagram, LinkedIn, and all the other social media which is now as fundamental to our daily lives as eating, we spent our dinners talking to our friends and family - listening to their day and their thoughts and their troubles and their joys. We showed them RESPECT by listening. Now we drag our iWhatevers everywhere with us and keep our faces attached to them permanently. Next time you are out and about at the grocery or to eat or Starbucks notice how many people are NOT paying attention to the person they are with or even the world around them at all. I think a sociologist would have a field day with looking at the ratio between some measure of respect and the amount of technology associated with a society. In 3rd world countries, it is necessary to be respectful to others so that you can get things done in your daily life. I would argue that is not as much a requirement in our 1st world society. The requirement for more personal interaction in less technologically advanced countries fosters the practice of being respectful as you go through your day: making phone calls or speaking with someone in person; going to a store to purchase instead of online; and the like. It is easy to text or email someone and have no interaction, no personal contact with the other person. When your mind views another person as merely an object, which I think happens when you do not have to directly talk/interact with them, then your mind also devalues that person some. And hence the decline of being respectful of that person, their time and their being.

How do we re-learn to re-spect each other? I am not sure but I know it has to start with getting out of our iBubbles and tuning back into WHO we are with and WHAT they are saying. And yes, I am EMAILING this to you, but with the utmost respect, trust me.

With very much love and respect for you taking the time to read this and humor me.....
Marny

Maybe next week I can lighten up a bit on being so down on everyone when I try to BE...specific. Ooooh I LIKE that one.

SPECIFIC

From: **Marny Jaastad** (marnymarie@yahoo.com)

To: evanmccleerybrown@yahoo.com

Date: Monday, November 11, 2013 3:58 PM

Evan:

Oh, I am so excited to challenge myself on this one. This is actually a very DO-ing type of BE. I can babble on f-o-r-e-v-e-r (yes, Marny I know; I've read your 43 other Be's and you drone on like a saw!) and not quite get to my point some times. I often find it necessary - in my mind - to give all kinds of background and reasoning and unneeded information before I ask/tell/state whatever it is I am actually getting at. I know I lose people along the way when I do that because I have come to notice when other people do this and I know they lose ME along the way.

So! Without further ado (already too much I know) let me just get right down to it! BE...specific!

In keeping with the nature of this week, I will be short and succinct. Not usually a strong quality of mine so this is quite the challenge. Essentially it boils down to not wasting someone else's time with your breath! A little harsh and crude, but true nonetheless. I have been very direct and to the point this week with people. I've also been trying to get a whole (bunch) of things moving forward with some other people so I've not had the opportunity to be long-winded! AND I have passed along this advice to others all week as well. That is likely my larger contribution to my goal to BE...specific. I didn't actually go so far as to STOP someone mid-sentence but I hinted that they might be able to provide less background and go right to the pith of their: question, story, lesson learned, anecdote.

The best thing that I did to BE...specific this week is going to have profound effects on some future ventures I hope! I sat my little self down and took out a binder and divided it into 4 parts - each a new "endeavor" that I am hoping to get going as I move away from my current job a little bit more. This has been great for me. Having it on paper, written down, each day making SPECIFIC goals and checking off that list! I am moving forward on two of the four projects already in just one week! And I have you to thank - very specifically! Haha

I will be done with BE...specific because there is no story, background, lesson learned or anecdote to add to it. Oh and it was my birthday and I had a fabulous day. Did SPECIFICALLY what I wanted to do and nothing else. Perfect.

Thank you from the bottom of my heart,
Marny

You will have to wait on what's up for this week as I am at work finishing this and will have to draw my next BE tonight or tomorrow........

RESOURCEFUL

Well hellloooo My Little Turkey!

Haha - it being Thanksgiving Week and all. Hope you are off from school all week and you can be VERY VERY resourceful about finding fun things to do.........to annoy your mom. HA!!

Woot! I get to call on my inner-MacGyver. You aren't old enough to know who that is but he was an action/drama TV guy "back in the old days." Anyway when he would get into a tough, seemingly inescapable position, he would either dig around and/or pull out of his pocket: a gum wrapper, a toothpick and a dime and suddenly he was exploding locks and busting through impenetrable doors. We loved MacGyver, he was the best. (In fact Wikipedia says this about the TV show: "The adventures of a secret agent armed with almost infinite scientific resourcefulness.") And so how apt that I choose him as my guide and mentor for this week of gettin' creative!

I always joke at work, because we have very LIMITED resources, that I have to MacGyver all of my exercises and workouts and the machines. So let's see if I can MacGyver my *mind* this week as well. I am still on my mission to get myself figured out by the New Year and to get some new balls rolling down the alley. How creative, clever and resourceful can I be? Find those resources, make 'em useful, Marny!

Annnnnd just today I had to call upon all of my resourceful powers to completely redo a program that I am presenting this coming Sunday. Two other people involved decided that they wanted me to go in a different direction than what I had thought we discussed. So after spending several hours preparing and being nearly ready to go.......WHAM! I was blind-sided with needing to come up with a whole new program and focus. I could have been combative and resistant and argued with them about what they wanted but I reminded myself that I AM resourceful and with that confidence I forged ahead, got my little brain to thinking, looked around the grocery store and my house for things that I already had to create some interesting snack for before and after kids exercise,

133

do activities, etc. My own personal practice of BE...resourceful went very well. Having the confidence to know that I had it in me to figure out a new plan helped so much more. BE...resourceful I kept telling myself.

I thought a lot about this one because there is a lot more to the art of Be(ing)...resourceful than simply looking around when you feel stuck. Really it is about being open-minded and letting your brain remove all of its usual constraints. We so often gravitate to what we know and do out of habit. Habit stifles resourcefulness. Simply having options in front of you is not enough. You have to open your brain to the possibilities that an object or person or thought can take shape and be used in a multitude of ways. Is a can opener always a can opener? Maybe not. It would seem that waking up that creative, open compartment in the brain is the first step to BE...resourceful. Finding yourself in a situation where you have to BE...resourceful is actually a great way to spice things up a bit and maybe give yourself and others a chuckle or two. Think about what you might do the next time it RAINS and you had planned to go to the park or ride your bike or.....what great indoor activity might you create? - NOT involving screen time - you might surprise yourself when you look around the house.

As I look around my home and think about the various standard uses for the things I have, I also noticed that I keep the funniest little bits of things. Wrapping paper, ribbon and ties, parts or pieces of broken items. I don't think I qualify as a hoarder yet (HA!) but I have always known that I was not a waster. I can't stand to throw anything away. And what do you know.......just when I had long thought that I was CHEAP, I am actually RESOURCEFUL! Without all of those little saved items I would not have the opportunity to BE...resourceful at a moment's notice.

Like I said, I can MacGyver anything. Now what did I do with that gum wrapper and clothespin......I need to fix a broken table leg.............

Much love and resourcefulness,
Marny

On to our next adventure. And a very appropriate follow-up...........BE...intuitive!

INTUITIVE

From: **Marny Jaastad** (marnymarie@yahoo.com)

To: evanmccleerybrown@yahoo.com

Date: Sunday, December 8, 2013 12:48 PM

Hi Evan!

I KNEW that this one was going to be next. Oh wait, that's not exactly what I am supposed to be doing, huh? No fortune-telling and palm reading for me this week. I will have to play crystal ball reader another time. Maybe next Halloween that will be my costume.

I have been a little blocked about what to write on this pensive nugget. I have been rolling it around my head every day - what does it really mean - why is this important in my life?

I DO know that trusting my gut is the way to go. My first inclination is typically the correct one - for me. How many times can you remember saying "I *knew* I should have picked that one, or stuck with that answer on a test, etc?" So the more times that happened when I was younger, it brought me to learn to trust my first instinct. I believe that there has also been actual science devoted to studying this. Go with your gut. But is that really being intuitive? It is a component of it certainly but I believe it goes deeper. Be...intuitive......
It's that time when you're watching the scary movie and the main character meets someone and gives that look of, hmmmmmm, maybe something here is amiss. And we, the audience, all know that this is the scary, "gonna chase you down and lock you up" character. The main character doesn't know this YET but can "feel" it from this person that they are bad news. Now of course the main character then gets themself into a situation where they do get taken away by the crazy person - and then they say "I *knew* there was something odd about him....." RIGHT! Trust your gut! Run the other way.

On a bigger life stage, there are times when having a hunch, or generally analyzing a situation and going with a decision or option based purely upon your emotional or perceptual read on it is the way to go. We tend to not trust our intuitiveness because we are SO inundated with studies and facts and science. We and others demand PROOF that something IS. Why is it not ok for the answer to be "because I can feel that this is true or right or wrong"?

136

We are taught to not trust our "feelings" - think with your head not your heart. Our society has become too focused on science and fact and made it harder to BE...intuitive. I think that it may also be that if we trust our instinct and intuition, then there is the secondary component of being "wrong"; of the perception of failing or not having something upon which to place blame. It's really not all that awful to be wrong or to fail. Great lessons are learned from failing and being wrong. You learn NOT to do it again - HEY and guess what????? That makes your intuition even BETTER the next time you come to a tough patch in your decision-making life. So risk it, follow your heart. Science and fact have their place - and provide input for your intuition - but nothing steers as well as your gut.

My heart tells me that I need to make some changes in my life. Take some risks, dip my toe in a lot of pools to test the temperature til I find one I like. I'm pretty sure it's the right thing to do, so I am just going to! I have no proof that this is my path, but I don't need it. Thanks for helping me to BE...intuitive. Did you know I was going to thank you? I bet you did......haha
love , Marny

And next week we begin our journey to BE...PRESENT! And I am pretty darn sure that this has nothing to do with Christmas!

PRESENT

From: **Marny Jaastad** (marnymarie@yahoo.com)

To: evanmccleerybrown@yahoo.com

Date: Saturday, December 21, 2013 6:19 AM

Hey Ev, Rock-Master Extraordinaire!

Wow this is so apropos for me right now. I am in UBER planning mode and making up all kinds of stories about what will be in the next few days, months and next year. So much so that I am missing out on RIGHT NOW. It's funny somehow because this is THE theme of yoga - be present. Be here be now because right now there is nothing more. It is such an odd concept for me, and for most Westerners I believe, as we are always moving FORWARD, striving for MORE, looking to the future. How many times have you heard, "What do you want to be when you grow up?" Only about 100, right? Well wait til you're 45 - old like me - and you'll be up to over 1000! And I STILL don't know. So much pressure about what is to COME. How about what I wanna be right n...o...w? I have a hard enough time with that.

Whew tough stuff. I admit it, I am "checked out" at work about 25% of the time right now. I have a BIG surprise trip this week - to see YOU as you already know by the time you get this - and so I am firmly in Seattle in my head already. I have to keep reining my brain back to BE...present. For my clients it is a matter of courtesy and it IS my job to pay attention to them. And more than that, for all of us to BE...present around others is just plain courteous. Think about when Mom picks you up in the car after school and asks, "What did you learn today?" or "How was your day?" Ugh....not again, seriously? It may seem so annoying and repetitive and you really just closed the door on school and you are already: at home, at Hady's, on your iPad, at practice, or where ever else but HERE AND NOW. Mom's not being annoying or nosey even - well when she starts to ask about the girls, THEN she's being nosey. HA! This is precious time to her - her HERE AND NOW with Evan. This little 10 minutes of time, just the two of you in the car, just BE...ing.

When we check out of a conversation - even with friends - we miss things that we can never get back. When you find yourself really practicing how to BE...present, it is that awesome feeling of "Where did the time go?" "How did it get to be so late?" It's that period when time does not matter nor does it exist. You are merely hanging out on this big old rock, hurtling through space and almost in suspended animation, the tick of the clock being irrelevant.

The benefits of challenging oneself to BE...present are many. I have learned it mostly through yoga over the past year. I had heard people at various stages in life mention the importance of not living in the past and future but here and now. Always sort of wrote it off. But in yoga I finally "got it." First of all, if I think about anything but what I'm doing right then, I fall over! It is the one place where I can "lose myself" I have found - pardon the pun (lost/found)! And I can attest that the benefits of that calming, non-planning, just BE...ing are immense. I know that there are actually health benefits to this as well. And many have commented on my more relaxed disposition. It's true, I believe. I am less agitated and crabby. I like myself better. Now THERE's a nice bonus outcome.

The future is always, the past is never but the present, to BE...present, is precious and is the only real, tangible existence we have. So channel your inner yogi and BE...present as much as you can each day. Oh, and I have to add that at Macklemore I was totally practicing how to BE...present. Nothing else mattered. I didn't think about when to go to bed, when I had to get up, what I was going to do the next day, or what I had done the day before. It was pretty awesome, thanks for going with me.

Love,
Marny

(I took Evan to his first-ever concert in Seattle. It was his surprise Christmas present. Macklemore and Ryan Lewis.)

And we move onto the future (haha) and how I am going to BE...active! Now that is truly hysterical. I never stop moving that is for sure. I think I will come up with a different focus for BE...ing active.

ACTIVE

Hello Evan.

Day after Christmas Chaos and I bet you are exhausted and the last thing you are thinking about is how to BE...active.....Well *you* only need to read about it; I will be doing the BE...ing.

Yah I already see it. BE...active, as in NOT passive. Don't let life pass you by my friend! And can you believe that this is our 48th BE?!?! (You were probably thinking that it was more like 100 years of it by now.) It's been nearly 1 year exactly since I began learning how to BE...so many different things. Wow. It has been quite a journey for me. I hope that you have found some of it interesting, thought-provoking or at the least somewhat humorous. I love writing to you and sending you my little thoughts and musings. I think we will be through our little bag of words around May. Not sure what I will have to dream up so that I can keep writing to you - and torturing you - but that's for another time.

I have set my course to BE...active for the next 2 weeks as directly as I can. I find it difficult to move forward with new things - it requires a lot of effort and energy - and sometimes I just want to sit and write to you. But no passivity for this gal! I have 2 projects that can be potential new jobs for myself that I am going to put effort into EACH DAY over the next 14 so that they move forward and I have some momentum. Inertia is a wonderful and a terrible thing. On the face of it to BE...active in our culture would tend to indicate physical activity. Get moving, get your butt off the couch. Turn off the screens! But I am taking my own liberties and using the property that a thing in motion tends to stay in motion and a thing at rest.....well, just sits there like a bump on a pickle!

I have been trying to diffuse this attitude out to others as well over this week. Get yourself going. Why sit and wait - and fret - about a decision or a situation in which you are troubled? BE...active in your life. Be a BE-er, not an idler. And people have embraced it. I can see that they have gained new energy and enthusiasm or courage to move forward, (to) push on. BE...active.

And I am also proud to announce that I have continued to move myself forward and BE...active in the progression of my life. Though it is always a struggle for everyone, rarely is the outcome of effort and focus not rewarded.

Change is: hard, scary and tough. People resist it by nature. YET, the irony is that on a nearly daily basis I hear at least one person say....."I'm bored with my life." Or "I'm not happy with my job." Or "this person always gets me in this bad situation and I end up saying yes to doing something I really don't like doing." And only a small percentage have the awareness to realize that NONE of these situations/events/relationships are static. They are dynamic and as such require activity to maintain that dynamism. BE...active and you live your life. BE...(not)active and it is lived for you. Your life should not live you; you should live your life.

That my dear Evan, is the name of The Game Life. Here is my realization from henceforth: BE...active equates to LIVING! (And in my case to my still most favorite BE ever....living your dreams)

love love love to you
Marny

And lucky number 49 will BE...optimistic! HA! And that is the perfect BE to follow BE...active. Because without the incentive and belief that the choices you make will have the outcomes you desire, how CAN you BE...active and move forward? Also quite a propos to the New Year and better things in 2014.

OPTIMISTIC

From: **Marny Jaastad** (marnymarie@yahoo.com)

To: evanmccleerybrown@yahoo.com

Date: Tuesday, January 7, 2014 6:20 PM

Dear Evan –

Wow this is going to be the BEST "BE" ever! Ok, I know, that's taking it a bit too far. But I have found out some interesting little tidbits about ME and maybe useful things for YOU going forward..........

So obviously this first week of the new year of 2014 is the perfect time to have BE...optimistic come up in my life. As I was lying in bed unable to sleep last night, I was thinking about being optimistic and my hesitancy to do so. What I realized is that with OTHERS, I am always very optimistic. Very much "look on the bright side" "every cloud has a silver lining", etc etc. I am forever the rose-colored glasses gal when it comes to others' lives. However, the irony is that with myself, it is the exact opposite. Absolutely. I usually joke that I am the eternal pessimist....that way you are never disappointed. Maybe in some odd little twist that IS being an optimist. I am however, always very, very hopeful that my pessimism will be wrong. What came to me in my non-sleep was that I am *protecting* myself by being pessimistic. I am so fearful of being disappointed that I "save" myself from that pain by having no expectations or low expectations. And voila, either I'm correct and not disappointed or I am pleasantly wrong. I am sure that this is a common defense mechanism for many people. It actually brought back to me your reaction about the "symphony" concert we went to. When you thought it was the symphony, you were less than excited. When you saw the Macklemore shirt, you couldn't bear the thought that it could possibly, maybe, the smallest chance be that we were going to that show because if you were wrong.,......oh the sadness!!!! (haha)

I conducted a very informal poll among others I know about this "protect yourself from disappointment" thing and all agreed. Yes, VERY positive when it comes to others - finding the good in a bad situation - but for themselves: gloom and doom. Sighhhhhh. So this past week I tried very diligently to embrace the positive, to BE...optimistic when faced with an uncertain situation. And hey - I think it actually worked a little. The most interesting part about my attempts to steer my attitude toward that of optimism was that I actually FORGOT about the "thing" over which I was worrying/expecting/anticipating. HUH! What I mean is that when I create the "worst outcome scenario", that behavior brings the "thing" to my mind MORE. Because I perseverate and worry about that horrible thing occurring. BUT when I decided to look at the situation from a positive perspective, to BE...optimistic about its outcome, I actually didn't give it a second thought! Wow, what a revelation. That of course left me with more time to BE...optimistic that I could accomplish more in the day and in life by testing out that scary, potentially disappointing act to BE...optimistic whenever I can be.

Try it out. Seriously. See if something arises this week that gets you into a worry-wart mode; "Oh no, what MIGHT happen?" "What I want to happen never will so I won't even think about it." Instead of those phrases try the opposite and see if it simply puts your mind to rest and you can completely forget about it and.............move on!

And so move on we do to the big old NUMBER FIFTY of our BE's..........
And so with great love and optimism, I leave you to ponder how we will BE...healthy and fit! HA!!!!!!!!!! I actually just laughed out loud. And you will see why.............next week.......when I come back at you healthier and fit-ter than ever.

Love, Marny

(For the Macklemore concert, I initially told Evan we were going to the symphony. Then I had him open a "dress shirt" box, which was a Macklemore t-shirt. He said, "You better not be kidding that we are going to this because that will be so mean!")

HEALTHY & FIT

From: **Marny Jaastad** (marnymarie@yahoo.com)

To: evanmccleerybrown@yahoo.com

Date: Tuesday, January 21, 2014 6:10 PM

Dear Evan - hope you're eating well and getting plenty of exercise and rest so you too can BE... healthy and fit! Hahaha

Which on the face of it seems oh-so-simple. Especially for a PERSONAL TRAINER! BUT! Ironically enough I launched my new business on Jan. 1 - My Fitness Gal. The premise of this business is that everyone defines FITNESS differently.

My focus this week has been upon being MENTALLY healthy and fit - tougher than it might seem! As I thought about and listed out the myriad ways there are to define healthy and fit, I realized that this changes for every person at different stages of their lives. And for some people it may change daily! To become a "whole" person, to BE...healthy and fit, requires incorporating so many things. Healthy could be: nutrition, exercise, psychological care. Fit could be: able to get through the activities of daily life or complete a marathon or have a baby.

However, I would say that to BE...healthy and fit comes down to one definition for everyone: BALANCE! You could actually spend your entire day wrapped up in trying to do all the "healthy" things that "they" (the omnipotent THEY) tell us to do so as to be "fit." But at the end of that day would you truly be healthy and fit? NO, you would be crazy, wrapped up in minutia and very much out of balance. Where was the learning? Where was the human interaction? Where was the BEing of humanness? Displaced by an obsession. Maybe we all need an exterior monitor so that we know when we have reached our perfect level of healthy and fit. Too much and then suddenly you are VERY unhealthy. When is that tipping point? When are you too fit? It would seem our brains do not have the capacity to determine the end point of that. There is always 1 more step to take. "If I just cut out sugar." "If I just do 5 minutes more of abs..." if if if.........
Why is it that our culture has so much fascination and obsession with trying to live forever? Do this, eat that, do this workout, take this class, don't eat that. It is beyond ever-present in our (daily) lives and particularly media. Lost is the art

of living healthfully and being fit FOR NOW. To enjoy this very moment in time. I'm not sure who came up with the idea that living longer would bring something better? Sure, it'd be nice to hang around a while longer but if you notice, no one is telling you WHY it will be so great to hang around a little longer. Personally I'd love to be around to see YOU more, to watch your life and (your) being emerge but that's selfish. If you were to ask people that is likely similar to what they would say as well.

BE...healthy and fit so you can live every single second - doing ALL the things that comprise your life, not merely the ones that create health and fitness - to its fullest.

So I hope that we can all find a *healthy* way to BE...healthy and fit. And moving into our last 19 BE's I really am amazed at the amount I have learned about myself. I know, I know I always say that. At least I'm consistent! And I don't lie....that MUST be healthy.....ha

Love, Marny

Here we go with 51, on my way to BE...loving! Well SHOOT it's not even Valentine's Day. Well I do know that I LOVE YOU! So there. I'm off to a good start. Maybe I'll scratch Wendy on the head or something too.

LOVING

Be...loving

From: **Marny Jaastad** (marnymarie@yahoo.com)

To: evanmccleerybrown@yahoo.com

Date: Wednesday, February 5, 2014 3:48 AM

I love YOU dearly, Evan.....

Every time I look up at my little stand with BE...loving, I automatically go "awwww" in my head. Good grief how silly! But it does make me smile every single time I look at it and it does make me want to be a little more caring and doting on someone. Oh the poor victim I encounter tomorrow.....will be loved to death. Aren't you so very happy you are in Seattle and not in SD!?

And certainly you can "love" pizza or "love" the Seahawks or "love" vacation.....but what is it truly to BE...loving? Versus to be IN love?
After I thought about how to BE...loving, I started watching others' behavior and actions toward the people they are close to in their lives. One of my dearest friends made a huge decision to choose between work and her boyfriend. The boyfriend won out. I was so proud of her for recognizing that the person that matters most to her in her life was not receiving any benefit from her working more hours. She put his importance in her life before her own agenda of work and income. In one sense to BE...loving involves a great deal of vulnerability. You have to "put yourself out there" and maybe not be received in the way that you wish by the other person. However, there is also a version of Being... loving which is pure and unconditional as when caring for a baby or a sick friend or someone who is emotionally fragile. That is also a selfless, altruistic act but with less vulnerability on the part of the "giver." There is likely not a fear of rejection of the love-giving and so it comes easily.

However, in the first case I noted to BE...loving is potentially scary and risky to your OWN emotional stability and health. It's a leap of faith taken from an intuitive sense. "Your gut" tells you that doing something selfless and caring for another is going to be ok. You will not be injured emotionally, you will be rewarded with a reciprocal love. Or so one hopes. The thing that is so wonderful when someone acts in a loving way is that there is absolutely no science or fact behind it. Our Western society shuns and belittles actions derived from emotions. But the strongest drivers we have in our bodies are our senses and our emotions. When an urge to do something loving for or toward someone arises, I would venture to guess that 90% of the time we quash that idea before it even fully develops.

The one exception is Valentine's Day. The day that anyone is given a "pass" on feeling silly for BEing...loving. In fact, just the opposite is true. People may chastise others for not embracing the "holiday" - Hallmark as its origin is. In my book every day should be Valentine's Day. Everyone needs a little loving every day. Some care, some compassion, a little pat on the head.
So when Alex is making you crazy because he is having a tough day or Jaden is playing prankster to the max, stop....take a deep breath.....and remember that deep down inside of you, somewhere in there, you can BE...loving to them. AND it just might work in a way that would surprise you. They may actually do exactly what you want them to do - stop a behavior, listen to what you are saying, play a game you want to play - without having to argue, fight or otherwise strong-arm them. So love 'em up!!!

As much as I love you to death, Evan. BE...a love now, will you go do your homework? Hahaha - ok, not quite the proper use but you know I love to make myself laugh.

Oh - one last thing. Send a little love your own way as well. When you hear that voice in your head telling you it's not good enough, fast enough, high enough, etc......BE...loving to YOU and ease off a bit. This is my biggest challenge every day. Stop the negative and start to BE...loving to ME!

Love (and I really mean it)
Marny

After all that love, I think I am seeing hearts everywhere......so let's move on to something concrete....BE...ACCOUNTABLE. Ooof! That's a tough one after all that self-love. Now a little self-CHECK!

ACCOUNTABLE

Dear Evan

Well it appears I slacked a little here - I am BEing...accountable for doing
that. How clever of me. I thought I wanted to ponder on this one a little more
and think about it but I feel pretty satisfied that I have chewed away on it
enough and incorporated some good lessons into my life. Just yesterday
someone "called me out" for something I had done that he didn't like. Though it
was completely unintentional and I could have reacted very defensively, I also
felt very badly afterward. I later went back up to him and said, "You were right.
I did something wrong and I am not going to excuse it or brush it aside. I
apologize and I thank you for bringing it to my attention as I will be more aware
of it from now on." And I meant it! And it actually felt good to "own up" to it
and be aware that we are responsible for our actions. So I guess it was good
that I held out a few more days to send this as I was able to put it into practice
and make myself a better person because of it.

"To be accountable means to be responsible or answerable to someone for
something. It involves taking responsibility for your own actions and being able
to explain them. Accountability comes in many forms and is used in all aspects
of our society," so says eHow. And so it MUST be!

Own it. Embrace it. Accept it. BE...accountable! Right...so why exactly is it so
important to be REMINDED to BE...accountable? Well I am going to go at the BE
from the other direction. Through the back door, one might say. I am going to
look at why people opt to NOT be accountable. To so quickly point the finger
elsewhere. To lie and deny. To claim ignorance and innocence. My gut reaction
is that they want "to avoid pain." Pain not being physical but mental and
emotional. That I get. Fessing up that you screwed up, that you made an error
in judgment, that you caused some misfortune IS truly painful, embarrassing
and possibly rife with some form of punishment. Oh but the punishment that
awaits when it is discovered that one is both accountable AND a liar. Eeek. We
all know it will happen....one lie begets another and another and soon the lies

154

have so tied themselves into knots that the prevaricator can never untie, nor find the original ends, of the knots. They trip, stumble and eventually are caught. And............have to BE...ACCOUNTABLE. Sheesh that's a whole lot of work to end up where you could have been to begin with.

Initially I was thinking that accountability comes into play more in the work world than in the living your life everyday world. (I did change my mind on that) But also that does not lessen its importance, nor the benefit to learning early-on to have ethics and integrity and own up to what you do. Even in the smallest of decisions. Because as you build your credibility by being accountable, people will look to you more and more as a leader, as someone "safe" whom they can trust. Never underestimate the power of trust in any relationship. Building trust is arduous. Breaking that same trust as simple as breaking a graham cracker. Accountability is more than mere honesty. More than raising your arm when someone asks," Who did....?" Accountability brings into the mix the need to practice conscious actions. To think before you speak or leap. Because if you do think first and choose an outcome or action that you believe in, can defend and will stand behind, then even if it is not necessarily a popular or even a wise action or course, you will be respected because you have been accountable, you have reasoned, supported and justified yourself. Be proud. Be unique in this world of scapegoating. BE...accountable!

Have a great day Evan. I hope that you can be proud and stand behind every decision and action that you take. Trust yourself and others will respect and trust you. I certainly respect and trust you.
Love, Marny

And now we will move to something a little less concrete maybe. BE...within your means........this is gonna be interesting.

WITHIN YOUR MEANS

Subject:	Be...within your means
From:	**Marny Jaastad** (marnymarie@yahoo.com)
To:	evanmccleerybrown@yahoo.com
Date:	Thursday, March 27, 2014 5:33 PM

Hi Evan, I have been thinking about you a ton lately.....missing you and remembering getting ready to visit you last April when you graduated and that most awesome of concerts I got to attend.

So for this BE, I am backing up from the end and putting "the end" at the beginning because this has, thus far at least, been my most difficult be. Until about two days ago I couldn't figure out WHY I was having such a hard time getting this one out of my brain and out to you. And then it hit me....hard.....kinda like a baseball upside the head with no helmet. OUCH! The reason I had been so resistant and procrastinating on completing this one was it forced me to look in the mirror! I had to point a finger at myself and ask, "Are you BEing...within your means?" You'll see more of what I am saying with this question as you read below. Suffice it to say that I am often on the very thin edge of not being within my means. Of almost but not quite toppling face first onto the ground. Somehow 99% of the time I am able to catch myself and the 99 plates spinning on the dowels around me. That doesn't mean it's a good thing that I can do that. Maybe I am lucky. Maybe I am skillful. What I do know is that I need to be more aware of and observant of my true "means" and to spend less time trying to push beyond them to some unknown, undefined other place.......and so it begins.....to BE...within your means.

Of course this is generally meant in terms of financial means. HOWEVER, it being Marny thinking about BEing...within your means, I am going in a whole other direction. Of course I am. I actually had a great awakening about this just recently. I injured myself in yoga, of all places, BUT it was because I did not pay attention to "my means" as in I stretched a little too far and injured my hamstrings. OUCH! Trust me. And so now I "pay the price" as they say. I have to rest and back off of "my edge" as they call it in yoga. In every class I take, teachers always talk about "the edge." It is that point where if you try to push or stretch or do a pose just a little deeper or challenge your balance a little more, you fall.....or pull a muscle......the edge is elusive and ever-changing, as our bodies are not the same day to day. Especially old people bodies!

One instructor described "the edge" this way:

"How far you can fold forward, for example, is limited by your flexibility edge; to go any further hurts and is actually counterproductive. The length of your stay in a pose is determined by your endurance edge. Your interest in a pose is a function of your attention edge. "

So how does one BE...within your means in the physical and mental life? It requires personal assessment. Knowing your abilities and limitations. Taking note of your state of mind and physical well-being.

"Don't bite off more than you can chew" an old, but still tried and true adage regarding how to BE...within your means. It means to be prudent and to assess your, well, assets and come to a rational conclusion as to whether you are able to take on a challenge or even a small task. Do I have what it takes? I used to constantly overbook/overwhelm/overdo my life. And I think this is something that people like your parents and you and me tend to do. We like to push the envelope, test our limits, raise the bar. And for the most part this is a great attitude and attribute to possess. As long as it's all done without making us completely crazy and spinning in circles, chasing our tails to complete our tasks.

I don't want you to ever lose that drive, determination and confidence that you possess in yourself, your skills and your abilities. Never second judge yourself. You know you and you are the best judge of you. I only want that you leave enough of "you" around for YOU to enjoy growing up and being with friends, family, or just yourself. Know your means, your limits, your outside edges. Push them every now and then to see if you have grown, expanded and can take on more. If you bounce off, take note and continue on, but if you break through, awesome. Know that you can still BE...within your means even if that MEANS holding back just a smidge.

Love you very much
Marny

I promise to be a little more prompt in getting my words to megabytes about our next BE...faithful.........my mantra.....oh look out you may get a book next time from me!

FAITHFUL

From: **Marny Jaastad** (marnymarie@yahoo.com)

To: evanmccleerybrown@yahoo.com

Date: Wednesday, April 23, 2014 3:28 AM

Dear Evan, to whom I am forever faithful

As I often do, I start with the "true" definition and move on from there.

First entry from a Google search is:

"loyal, constant, and steadfast."

Nexy entry is :

"having a strong belief in a particular religion, esp. Islam"

Yup, that is exactly what came to mind when I began to think about how to BE...faithful. For my own practical purposes, as in how I will instill faithfulness in my week or life, I am going with choice A since I really don't have a specific religion to which I subscribe. Though I do certainly respect and acknowledge that it is a very important part of being faithful. I was put into a perfect situation to trust my faithfulness as a friend this week. My friend and someone I work with is unhappy at our company. She asked to talk with me this past week and told me she is being recruited by another gym that is very nearby to us and is obviously a competitor. Of course she has not yet said anything to our management as they would certainly ask her to leave. Now I have two allegiances here: employer and friend. How to BE...faithful? Of course there was not truly a choice for me - my friend would "win out" without even a moment's hesitation. But as she was revealing all of this to me, there was this slight, nagging voice in the back of my head......"Do I mention something to our boss?" "To someone else in our group of trainers to let THEM tell the boss?" I will do neither as I do not see this as any threat to the company. But when might my faithfulness (or loyalty) fall toward the company? If there were some sort of threat of injury to an individual or a breach of a contract or an unethical act going on, I would have to think seriously about betraying the trust my friend had put in me. If she were starting a directly competing business on her own or if she was using confidential company information to further outside interests, I would feel the scale tipping toward my employer. BUT I would also be very open and clear with her that this was information that I felt I had to pass along and that it might be in her best interest to do so prior to me ratting her out!

So how would I define the difference in my attachment, as it were, to my friend or to my employer? I came to the conclusion that one is *loyal to* some people/organizations and one is *faithful to* others. I think loyalty is always a component of faithfulness but not vice versa. Faithfulness can be a component of loyalty but not 100% of the time. Subtle but important in making my decision, or let's say in other decisions such as this where you might be given information and feel conflicted as to how to deal with it. And then beyond this difference of loyalty and faithfulness comes the fact of human nature to want to *tell* someone about interesting or "juicy" information. To gossip. This is a topic for another BE I think but it is relevant here in that the urge to spill your guts is certainly quelled by faithfulness. The pain, anger and repercussions of committing that betrayal to your confidante far outweigh any gain you might get from divulging the information.

Faithfulness implies longevity, time, and shared history. It is about riding the roller coaster of life with someone and remaining by their side even in the rough patches. It means not turning away when you are emotionally hurt or harmed by someone or by their words or actions. And we remain faithful because the reward of the relationship is those times when you reach the top of the hill on the roller coaster and your stomach drops for just a second in anticipation. You get that feeling of excitement, energy and elation at how wonderful it is to be with that person.

So for me, to BE...faithful is about being in it for the long haul. It is about ironing out the wrinkles that arise in the fabric of living day to day with people you care about.

Just like Tucker (Evan's dog) is EVER faithful to you. I am as well faithful to you forever, Evan.
Love, Marny

And faithful as I have been to the writing of our BE's, next week I will explore how to BE...playful! Awesome! I can get back on that roller coaster theme! Haha

PLAYFUL

From: **Marny Jaastad** (marnymarie@yahoo.com)

To: evanmccleerybrown@yahoo.com

Date: Wednesday, May 21, 2014 5:34 PM

Evan! I must have been slacking off and PLAYING too much since it has taken me forever to get this off to you. Sheeesh! Sorry. So play we have come to. Why do I need to BE...playful I asked myself? Hmmm maybe because of the number of times that people tell me to take myself LESS seriously? To "chillax"! To "roll with it." Play it turns out is actually a basic human necessity. Like air, water and nutrients. I have this on record from none other than myself.

Turn on Animal Planet and (you will) find all kinds of examples of primitive playing. Play is innate. It is a basic instinct in all beings - human and animal. Why is that we are so drawn to "play." It is a release. It makes us feel good. It provides a way to interact in a pleasant way with others. So many more reasons as well. However, I really think that as life has become more fast-paced, more intense, more pressurized, PLAY has become both lost and missed in our society. The expansion of the digital, plugged-in, 24/7 life has led to an existence on a train that has no depots or stations. We now can, and DO, keep in motion constantly. More so in a mental/intellectual capacity than in a physical way. Play then becomes even more important for that physical outlet and for the letting go of the intellectual. The constant processing. The brain in perpetual motion.

For adults play is often looked down upon and seen as frivolous. One researcher has actually found that "lack of play was just as important as other factors in predicting criminal behavior among murderers in Texas prisons." YIKES! Get me out on the merry-go-round stat! Play is also universal. There really is no need for any language in play. Sure we use it to describe "rules" of a game or to call out to each other if tossing a ball or frisbee. But we can play just as easily through sign and body language. You could play pick-up soccer in Seattle as easily as Spain. (Well you'd have to get on a plane first, I realize.) I did really challenge myself to make my day and my job more playful. People come to me for release. Physical and mental release. And sometimes my workouts can seem like a job. So I have reminded myself that sometimes we need to be silly and let our bodies and minds simply playout rather than workout!

With that said, there's a Twister Game on the floor that's calling my name. Haha. Have a fabulous play day. Hoping that I can come over to play at the McCleery Brown house soon,

xoxo
Lots of playful smooches and hugs
Marny

I'm not sure we can top playful but next up I will work on my skills to BE...TENACIOUS! That's a great one for me.....like a dog with a really really meaty bone.

TENACIOUS

From: **Marny Jaastad** (marnymarie@yahoo.com)

To: evanmccleerybrown@yahoo.com

Date: Sunday, May 31, 2014 6:12 AM

Dear Evan,

I think that my year and a half of torturing you with the weekly-ish "BE's" definitely meets my quota for BE...tenacious! Oh yes. This is a trait which Marny can excel at exhibiting. To the point of irritation on the part of others. The boundaries of tenacity and the point at which tenacity becomes....what? Obsession? Short-sightedness? Dangerous-ness maybe? We as a Western society are "driven" from a young age - as I'm sure you can agree! "Push beyond your limits, never give up, keep your eye on the prize." How often do we hear phrases and words such as this as we are growing up? (And even AS grown-ups......though I still wonder when I won't *feel* like I'm still in the growing up phase) But that is another BE.

To BE...tenacious teaches follow through, dedication and goal-mindedness. It is interesting to me that we feel the need to "teach" these traits. If this is not a naturally occurring tendency in humans, why do we find it to be so important? We definitely cultivate the behavior in our society. I guess you could argue that babies do exhibit tenacious behavior - ever hang out at someone's house with a hungry baby around? Uh huh. Those little beings can wail for hours it seems when hungry/tired/in need of changing. Tenacity indeed.

Tenacity is all heart. Or at least it's one of those attributes we ascribe to the heart. It's the childhood story of, *"The Little Engine That Could,"* translated into action. But taken too far tenacity becomes irritating and detrimental to one's goals. As in "extremely or objectionably persistent: a pertinacious salesman from whom I could not escape," according to Wikipedia.

As important as it is to stand up for yourself and your beliefs, it is also important to know when to "back down" as they say. Trying time and time again to get a friend to do an activity they clearly do not want to do may in the end harm the friendship more than the value we believe that friend might gain from the experience. Not everyone enjoys the challenges and activities that we find pleasurable. Though we may wish to convince them that skydiving is the best thing since Nutella, they just aren't buying it.

To BE...tenacious is to be passionate and driven and focused. Tenacity can take us far in life. Up the ladder of success, over the rainbow to the pot of gold or leaping tall buildings in a single bound. And while individual success as a result of being tenacious is awesome and so important, along the way, we must be wary to not knock someone else off the ladder, or miss the view from atop the rainbow (on the way to the pot of gold of course!) or bypass the scenic route in favor of getting there as fast as you can.

I hope you have a very successful baseball season this year. YOUR tenacity certainly has come through for you in this sport and in many other parts of your life. Embrace that tenacity. But remember there are a few roses along the way that you can stop to stick your nose in and breathe deeply. THEN you can leap over the building in a single bound!

I will always BE...tenacious in my attempts to share my thoughts and "wisdom" with you. I love you so much Evan. You are very special and I enjoy hearing about and watching as you grow up to be an amazing person.

Love, Marny

And on deck next for action is to BE...reliable!

RELIABLE

From: **Marny Jaastad** (marnymarie@yahoo.com)

To: evanmccleerybrown@yahoo.com

Date: Thursday, June 26, 2014 4:24 AM

Dear Good Old reliable Evan! (haha)

The word reliable has its origins in *relier,* Old French for "fasten" or "attach." I've been trying to figure out over the past weeks as I pondered about and tried to BE... reliable how we got to our definition of reliable from fasten or attach. Fasten and attach can connote security. To fasten TO or attach TO something secures it. I'm borrowing a little math theory here....by the transitive property then, being reliable brings security (to others??) or maybe security of mind. But I have gone a more literal route with my feelings on reliability since it is something that I pride myself upon in my own life.

This is a BE for Tucker! Talk about reliable. Always to be counted upon for love, affection, loyalty and protection.

It's funny because as I look back on my various "jobs" and stages of life, I would say the one thing that people have always said about me is that I am reliable - in one way or another. Someone said, "We know what we're going to get from you every day" (rowing coach). Another employer gave me the only key to the building other than theirs (the gym I work at now).

There would seem to be no downfall to having the tag "reliable" attached to your name BUT with it, I have found a measure of guilt or more accurately an obligation, to *maintain* that quality. There are days when maybe I just don't want to be relied upon to be at the gym early or to take a specific class or to do "my usual." In my world, reliability and routine are intertwined. I wonder if that means that to BE...reliable one cannot also BE...spontaneous?!?! Or BE...sporadic. Though they may not be mutually exclusive, it would seem difficult to rely upon someone who may be sporadic in their actions or words.

Early in one's life I think it is important to learn and develop the skills that garner the reputation of being reliable. Better to start "safe" so to speak and toe the line for the most part and show up every day in everything you do with consistency and dependability. As we get older and find more of who we are and what we believe, we can stray a little from the routine, away from "this is

169

who Evan is and what we can count on him to do" more toward a little surprise every now and then.

In the end I would certainly vote to BE...reliable and to be considered as such. That is my personality. That is also my need - to FEEL needed and useful and RELIABLE.

You know, Evan, that you can ALWAYS rely on me to be there for you whenever you need me, or DON'T need me (then I'll leave you alone, promise). I guess in your world I am reliable to always come up with an interesting gift or find fun "stuff" to do.

I hope that you will embrace all the good to be found and be respected when you are told to "BE...reliable".

Love, Marny

See you in a week!!

 And at that point, I'll have been working on how to BE...forward thinking!

OY! That's a toughie for me! No more ruing the past – for at least a week or so (haha)

FORWARD
THINKING

From: **Marny Jaastad** (marnymarie@yahoo.com)

To: evanmccleerybrown@yahoo.com

Date: Friday, July 11, 2014 3:52 PM

Dear Evan,

Well let's jump right into FORWARD THINKING. Here we are at number 58. Only 14 BE's to go. I am always surprised when I pull the next one of out the bag and see the word or phrase. I keep thinking, "Haven't we gone through all of the good, positive, constructive attributes and actions that ARE? By the end of the summer, you and I will have BECOME so many different things over the course of the last year and a half. I know I'm a better and different person for it. I of course always hope that you have gained maybe one tiny little bit of insight/interest or intrigue from one or more of them.

I realize and recognize that I do spend a lot of time looking back. Ruminating, revisiting and sometimes ruing what has occurred before. "If only..." "What if I'd..." "Argh! Just this or that and we would have won..." My newest favorite phrase for myself and the world is: "There's a reason why the rearview mirror in your car is so small compared to the windshield. There's a lot more ahead of you than behind you."

So here's the funny thing about forward thinking, which I of course "Googled up." In the mainstream, it's about finding the better widget. Those who are forward thinking favor innovation and development. They are progressive. A visionary. Well THAT is certainly far from my initial attempt at BEing...forward thinking. However, I would like to go with that and see where it takes me. Having just returned from seeing you and your family in Seattle, I as always, have all of you on my mind. And more specifically, I have "how do I get to see MORE of you" on my mind. That may not be of such great importance to you right now. But maybe in the future it will be more appealing. As I was walking to the grocery store today I was thinking about you and Mom and your friend on the cruise and how really awesome that must be. I wish I had been able to figure out how to join you but alas.....work. So my slant on how I am going to BE...forward thinking is to create a better way to see you more. I realize that there is no magic formula for this. I simply need to *create* the time and ability to do so. I think it is so difficult for all of us – no matter our age – to grasp that time is fleeting. We cannot "get back" events or moments or time that has gone by. The person who figures that one out is TRULY a visionary, the ultimate innovator. Ok I'm getting a little off track and silly here.

My goal over the next year, or before next summer, is to BE…forward thinking enough to develop a plan that will achieve my ultimate goal of our #16 BE…living your dreams. A plan to spend more time in Seattle with your family.

But for the present time, I have tried to BE…forward thinking at work. You have to figure that a gym is a gym is a gym, right? How innovative or visionary can you be with simply working out? I'd like to think that the answer is as many as you can wrap your brain around. At work I have tried to build that better mousetrap. I am always thinking about ways that I can approach my training sessions from a different perspective or with a different theme. Of course I utilize all of that innovative, NEW equipment and toys that are always being brought into the world of exercise and fitness.

But I also think that to BE…forward thinking requires a mindset that can be learned. UCDS (Evan's school) is one of those places that teaches kids (and adults I think!) how to think differently. Around, out of, next to and completely separate from THE BOX. Education like this that nourishes and fosters different solutions is invaluable. When I hear about the projects and such that you and Jaden and Alex do, I am amazed, intrigued and more than just a tad jealous. So far from my k-6 grade experience. I promise I am NOT going down the "you just don't know how fortunate you are" road.   But I am quite interested to see how this background sets the 3 of you up for the rigors of life. I believe that you will be innovative, creative, visionary and FORWARD THINKING in all that you do. You will be the "go-to" people in college, work life, family life.

Enough with the fortune telling. But I was being forward thinking…..with a little liberty. I will continue on my path to BE…living my dreams via my current challenge to BE…forward thinking.

Hope that Alaska cruise was truly one of the more inspiring things that you have done in your life.

Lots of love as always,

Marny

We are off on a new challenge to BE…content. OOF! Didn't see that one coming! Guess I don't get to complain that I can't be on that cruise with you and Mom…..I'll BE…content to sit here and watch Wendy chase her tail.

CONTENT

From: **Marny Jaastad** (marnymarie@yahoo.com)

To: evanmccleerybrown@yahoo.com

Date: Tuesday, July 22, 2014 3:05 AM

SIGH! I think that is the appropriate way to begin a week of how to BE...content. I am going to try to make this BE another experiential one. As in each day (or so?) I will try to remind myself in some situation to BE...content. With how hard I work, how much I read, how much I clean my house, who I am....whatever the situation that arises where I hear that little voice on my shoulder asking..."Could you do more? Is that enough?" Just BE...content with where you are, Marny!

One of my yoga teachers often intones the idea of "you are enough" at the start of our practice. Enough (of) what you may ask? Just....enough. We are a society of bars and lines and goals and contests and stretching limits. To BE...content with your status in the world, is quite tantamount it often seems to being lazy! Logically I can see the silliness in that. But my competitive brain and spirit push me ever further. More, higher, faster, longer, stronger, smarter.......

I don't have a spectacularly good story from the past 10 days or so to demonstrate how to BE...content. Though in several situations over that time the phrase did pop into my head and I said to myself....."so there you go. BE...content." Do not attempt to do more or regret the outcome or wonder if only. And it definitely allowed me the freedom to let go of that pattern and move onto something that maybe I could still affect.

But what I *did* think about often was you and your un-baseball summer. This is likely not going to be a super popular position for me to take with you but here goes. As I was walking one day and thinking about you and Mom and Maine and the cruise it occurred to me that your situation this summer with your injury and the consequent not playing as much as you wanted to, not taking the trip to Cooperstown, not making it as far as you wished in All-Stars was a great example of a BE...content situation. I am in no way saying that you should "settle" - which is far different from being content - rather that once you did all that you could do, in the moment, as you did, the outcome cannot be changed. Inasmuch as you can, BE...content with the outcome of all of your hard work over the past 9 years. It did bring you to this point of great success, even if that success had great disappointment! Every time you were thrown for a loop, you charged headfirst right back in. Pinch hit? You bet! Learn to run faster? Check! Get better at bunting? Done! Had you been able to catch and throw with your teeth, I have no doubt you would have. And you would have been successful at it to boot!

I am not trying to belittle or downgrade the level of disappointment and heartache at the outcome of your little league experience. Trust me, I know well the frustration and pain of the almost there, the silver medal, the runner-up. But I also know that when I look back at those near-misses, I can BE...content in the knowledge that I more than "just showed up." I battled and fought and got up again and again to do the most I could do with the situation I found myself in. And in that moment, I console myself with the fact that "I am enough" winding back to my yoga teacher and her wisdom.

Evan, I hope you too can BE...content at some point in the future. Maybe in the fall, maybe next summer, maybe in 5 years, with the fact that you too, are enough. You never give in, you give it your all + 10% and you are always successful no matter the outcome.

I am envisioning you lying in the lake in Maine, floating around, thinking about nothing in particular except maybe what you will get for your birthday next week and some really good tasting lobster!

Love and contentment,
Marny

Now launching past our contentment, let's see what I can learn to BE... this coming week. BE...empathetic! Oh how I feel your pain. And we're off.......

EMPATHETIC

Subject: Be...empathetic

From: **Marny Jaastad** (marnymarie@yahoo.com)

To: evanmccleerybrown@yahoo.com

Date: Thursday, August 14, 2014 4:53 AM

Dear Evan,

I can totally relate to your disappointment this summer about baseball.....and so begins my challenge to BE...empathetic. I've had equally frustrating/disappointing/painful injuries that sidelined me from great goals.

On the surface of it, I first thought that this is a pretty common "ability" for most humans. Except that what I realized is that (with) people what passes for empathy with another, is someone trying to demonstrate how their pain/anguish/catastrophic situation deserves greater acknowledgment? Example: someone says, "Oh you will never believe what happened to me...." and launches into some story about traffic and kids fighting and groceries falling out of the bottom of the bags. Their "friend" says, "Oh I totally know what you mean! I blah, blah blah...." And proceeds to tell their own story - of course made to sound 1000 times worse than the first person's tale of woe - so as to indicate how much more horrible their toil through life is.

Empathy? NOT!

So then what does it mean to BE...empathetic?

To the letter it means to have the understanding of someone else's situation because YOU have experienced that situation. With that in mind can any of us really be empathetic? I think no. Another quote came to mind...."unless you've walked in their shoes" you don't know how someone else feels.
The other interesting thing about empathy is that it really is directed toward BAD experiences. Of course the similarity/relationship to SYMpathy cannot be overlooked.

The things that we can certainly be most empathetic about are emotions. We can all identify with I'm scared. I'm nervous. I'm excited. I can't wait. These are the things where we can truly say. "Oh I so know what you mean!"

Your shoulder injury actually provides you the exact experience that allows for empathy. You CAN truly say you have empathy for someone when they experience great disappointment and frustration, sadness and anguish. All those feelings you felt when you were told you couldn't throw for 3 months. The quick mental summation of your plans for the summer (halted), your goals for baseball (sidetracked?) your hopes and dreams (dashed). BUT in the end there was also HOPE: you got to pinch run - and show off your hard work spent getting faster this year. You got to remain with your team to the final game. You were able to try out different things over the summer - working with preschoolers??!? Who knows what these experiences might bring to you in the future.

So when you have a friend or even one of your brothers who goes through a similar situation, you can really say, with all honesty: "Boy do I know how you feel. And let me share with you what great things happened for me as a result of that abrupt change in my plans." You will know that ache in your heart feeling, the anger, frustration, sadness, all of it and you can provide the comfort to them that worked for you.

Empathy is a sentiment that brings people together. Unity over a common experience/feeling. The "I'm-not-the-only-one" statement when two people realize that life can be just as unfair to others as to oneself......or that it can bring forth new options and opportunities as a result of the sharing of the empathetic stories.

I hope your summer did bring you happiness and peace of mind in the end and that you are excited for whatever new experiences will arrive this school year. Remember how you felt both at the beginning and end of the summer and use that to help comfort someone else when they struggle through a tough time. Love, Marny

Moving on to a little more upbeat stance, we will next learn to BE...constant.

CONSTANT

Subject: **Be...constant**

From: **Marny Jaastad** (marnymarie@yahoo.com)

To: evanmccleerybrown@yahoo.com

Date: Monday, October 20, 2014 4:32 PM

Dear Evan!

An interesting one to try to BE. So many roads that one could take with this. To be constant is to BE...faithful, devoted, attached, true.

It is also to "conform to or follow rules exactly."

It is NOT what I have been. Though I have thought about it many times. This BEing...constant. I have written nothing in a month! And now it is TWO months.

Ok now this has simply become ridiculous. The fact that I have become hung up and stuck on BE...CONSTANT is more than a little ironic to me.
I can sit down and make a series of lists as to WHY I have not been constant in my doling out of BE wisdom on the (mostly) weekly basis of the past but I think what I really want to tell you is that to BE...constant might not be all it's cracked up to be.

This could be my first to BE or NOT to BE pontification.

Don't get me wrong, I am still the most constant, steadfast, reliable, always-there-Marny that I have forever been. I will always be that way. It is my nature. I like for people to know that they can depend upon me and know that they will be pretty assured of getting the same person every day. Doing the same things to the best of her abilities.

HOWEVER. It has been a fall full of UNconstant things. I got injured and had to go on crutches - well that certainly changed my life. Ironically, the constancy of my workouts in particular is exactly what LED TO the injury. So much for constancy and health. Of course part of the constancy is being mindful of and true to my body, which obviously needed a rest for a little bit. Something I KNOW you can identify with after The Summer of the Shoulder.

I had major dental surgery which changed my ever-constant diet. Though the irony here is also that I have now adopted another constancy in my new diet. Even more bland and boring than before!

Basically, my normal, "never been in the hospital or ever had anything wrong with me" life was gone. What I was used to as being constant in my life - guaranteed health, fitness and maybe even a hint of being invincible was gone. POOF! (ok, not quite poof, but at least a strong pffft with thumb on nose.)

But I forge ahead. I continue to work as though nothing is different. I have creatively cobbled together some pretty effective workouts I can do and maintain the need to feel active. So although it seems that my life has abruptly stopped its constancy, I would have to look back now and say, "Well maybe this is the new constancy." For now. All of this will heal and be behind me and maybe when I return to BE...constant, I will employ a different definition. Maybe "following rules and conforming exactly" is situation-dependent. We will see. This exercise in BEing....has gotten me to think a lot. It's allowed me to chat at, if not with, you and has opened some new possibilities in my mind and world.

To BE...constant is so broad. As a friend, I am without fail, ALWAYS THERE. For you, as I hope you know, I am ALWAYS THERE. I am loyal and loving and available at the drop of hat for any and all who need me. Constantly.

Love
Marny

I guarantee that I will not be so lackadaisical in my exploration and pursuit of how to BE...professional!
THIS is right up my alley.

PROFESSIONAL

From: **Marny Jaastad** (marnymarie@yahoo.com)

To: evanmccleerybrown@yahoo.com

Date: Wednesday, November 12, 2014 3:24 AM

Dear Sir: (nice professional greeting!)

This is the foundation for all that I have ever done in any of my jobs. BE...professional. It says more than a dictionary worth of words about how you conduct yourself, your respect for others and for yourself and your work.

And this BE arrives at a perfect time as there are many strains upon us at work and it is very easy to be UNprofessional at times with all of the chaos we have amid a major renovation project.

But seriously, why in the heck should a 13 year old even CARE about how to BE...professional??? It's not like you are putting on that three-piece, grabbing your briefcase and jumping on the highway. BUT I would argue that in many instances, your "workplace" is school and taking on the qualities that one would expect in that environment to BE...professional will get you just as far as doing so at a traditional "job."

My argument for YOU to BE...professional derives from the fact that, as sad as it is, our society judges people by first impressions. We make split-second (unconscious) decisions about the level of respect deserved and status of someone based upon a nanosecond interaction........(if you want to read some amazing stuff about this, see Malcom Gladwell's book, *Blink).* It's almost frightening how our unconscious mind sorts through terabytes of data in a first impression to come to a conclusion before we can even consciously recognize it.

SO! Just **how** might you, Mr. McCleery Brown, BE...professional??? This is my little primer on school and professionalism....there will be no test I promise.

1. Realize that getting feedback on your work – even critical feedback – is part of the job; it's not personal. Getting angry or defensive or otherwise taking it personally when your teacher gives you feedback can be an easy trap to fall into. Your teacher is not trying to make you feel badly, they are trying to help you in your job of learning. If you see your teacher as someone whose job is to enforce rules, spoil your fun and make you do things you don't want to do, it will show – and it won't look good.

2. Dress to impress. Even though school may not have a uniform you have to wear I think it actually makes a difference in how you feel at school if you dress to look "nice" versus just this side of pajamas.

3. The three R's: Responsible, Respectful and Reliable. Don't curse in classes or around any one older than you. Try not to curse at all. And I know it's hard when you are frustrated and you've heard adults using foul language to not just let the swears rip. But it really turns people off - I have been "called out" as an adult for my tendency to have a foul mouth! Especially if you're in an argument, keep a calm, firm tone not raising your voice and yelling. If you tell your teacher or friends something, see it through. If you're honest, they will be more likely to rely on you and respect you.

4. Do your work. In class, make sure you get your work done. At home, get your work done (even those chores).

Ok lesson over, class dismissed. I know it seems ridiculous and dumb to think about these things at 13 but if you practice this behavior now, it becomes second nature in the future and without even realizing it, you are always seen as the epitome of how to BE...professional!

Gee that was a heavy one. Next week let's see if we can lighten up a little bit with how to BE...boundless!

Well. That certainly could be the opposite side of professional!

Love, Marny

BOUNDLESS

From: **Marny Jaastad** (marnymarie@yahoo.com)

To: evanmccleerybrown@yahoo.com

Date: Thursday, December 25, 2014 6:16 PM

Dear Evan,

Here we are at the 2 year mark since you present-ed (get it? haha) me with this awesome BE. It may by this point be your greatest regret in gift choice but it has provided me such a special and unique chance to see my life in other ways and to share some of me with you.....but onto the subject at hand.

Somewhat ironic to move from how to BE...professional to now putting my brain in what seems to me the other direction to BE...boundless!
Each time I have started to ponder how to BE this way the first connection that came to mind was regarding energy! How can I find boundless amounts of energy?? But being boundless goes far beyond the mere physical ability to DO more. As I have found over the last nearly two years of learning how to BE different things, it is the MENTAL component that is fundamental to embracing a new way of BEing. And that could not be more true than with this BE.

Boundaries, bounds, borders.....so many words in our language and thoughts to create a "box" or a container or an "end" to something. It seems so necessary for us to have the "outer limits" of something defined. Why might that be? So that we can achieve those outer limits? So that we feel safe in knowing that there IS an outer limit; that certain events or feelings or experiences might not go on forever or with no known endpoint?

As I think about how I can BE...boundless I must first examine my day -to-day existence. My routine, my habits, my patterns of living. And my need for having bounds and safety and comfort in the knowledge of the "edges" of my world. What would it be to wake every day with no boundaries? To let instinct and the wind - as they say - blow me where ever it took me. It's a little existential but certainly worth the exploration and thought process behind it. I contemplate this more to release me from the structure and "have to" of my typical life than to think what might be from this release.

I do many of the things in my life because "that's what I do." I go to work at 4am, because "that's what I do." As I have recovered from the injury I had several months ago with my leg, I have tried to be boundless in the options available to me for getting strong again and for resuming the activity that I enjoy so much - running. The activity that ironically brought on the injury. I have opened myself up to other options to achieve the same physical and mental release that I find in running and have been pleasantly surprised to have "un-bound" myself from my previous schedule and regimen. (From) "If it's Monday, I must be running 8 miles on the treadmill...." To "what does my body feel like it can do today?"

This (Christmas) morning, as I was pondering how to finish up this somewhat amorphous BE, I thought about a waffle. Yes, really. A waffle with all of its little compartments and how when I eat a waffle, I try to get butter and syrup into EACH of those boundaries. Because there is a boundary it must be filled! So I decided that maybe for this coming year, 2015, I might try to be a little more of a pancake than a waffle. Kind of let everything slide all around, cover what it covers. I think I'll find out that it all tastes the same in the end, no matter how I get there, so taking the approach to BE...boundless might yield a more interesting trip each time I embark on something that seems routine and restricted. Getting from A to B might be the goal but the path is really the part that is most interesting.

I hope that all of the paths you start down are filled with boundless amounts of fun, challenge, curiosity, and surprises but ultimately reward and happiness. Love you BOUNDLESSLY!
Marny

As we move along to our last 9 BE's there are still plenty of life's lessons to be learned and experienced and practiced. Next on our personal growth challenge....how to BE...romantic. WHOA didn't see that coming. Oh great, just what you need, some old chick telling you how to meet girls......hahaha

ROMANTIC

From: **Marny Jaastad** (marnymarie@yahoo.com)

To: evanmccleerybrown@yahoo.com

Date: Tuesday, January 21, 2014 6:10 PM

Ah yes...romance, love, passion, devotion. Romance is most definitely one of those things that is in the eye of the beholder.....or the receiver.

This is a tough BE for me since I am currently single! I am certainly not going to dote on Wendy! But nonetheless I know what I have found to be romantic over the years when I was dating people and also just from watching others interact with each other and thinking......"Awww that's so nice."

I will give you my view on romance and love over the years I have experienced it and let you pick and choose at your own will what might feel right and work for you. It's never too early to start to think about this stuff ya know!

From my standpoint it comes down to five simple things:

 *** stir someone's intellect – show an interest in things in which they have an interest. Be adventurous in your exploration of the world and the matters of the brain. Engaging someone mentally is as alluring as holding a hand or touching a cheek.

*** open doors – ALWAYS; not much else to say here; ANY door: car, building, taxi, restaurant.

*** walk on the street side of your dearest; this is a little left over from the days of chivalry and knights and all but I still like it. It conveys protection and caring and safety to me.

*** nothing wrong with a rose now and then - for no reason at all. Or better yet a poem or a letter saying simply WHY you care about someone.

*** practice saying I love you - and mean it. Learn to look someone directly in the eye and say I....LOVE.....YOU.

How you achieve each of these romantic gestures is varied and what makes each of us able to show our true selves. Spontaneous, unexpected "out-of-nowhere" actions are the heart (pardon the pun) (of) how to BE...romantic.

Why in particular for men, I believe, is it so difficult to BE...romantic? Vulnerability? Embarrassment? Discomfort? Fear? All of the above I would guess. It is definitely somewhat tricky to be romantic without feeling corny or insincere. The thing to remember if you are interested in someone, or are dating someone, is that inside our brains we are all very similar. The fear/vulnerability/unease that goes with putting yourself out there is not unique to the male species, or to you. A leap of faith can sometimes lead to the greatest thing that ever happened to you.

As a final note, maybe it's because it is the new year, or maybe because romance and love have been on my mind since choosing this BE but I definitely have noticed my interest in dating/meeting people to have increased in the past month. Coincidence I think. I also have noticed I want to play matchmaker for my clients more!

As we move toward February and Valentine's Day, take a moment to think about what YOU would find romantic from someone else. It is likely that they would also find that to be romantic coming from you.

Yes, I will be done with the sappiness now. I can't wait to watch as you have your first dates and "love interests." And if you will, to share some of those experiences with me.

 Love,

Marny

Next on our ever-intriguing plate of BE-ness is how to BE...a friend!!! Almost as good as how to BE...romantic. This might be its very own book in and of itself!

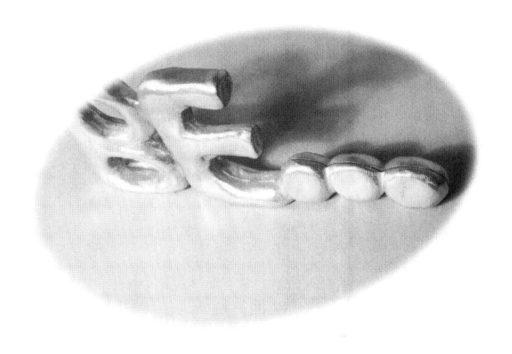

A FRIEND

From: **Marny Jaastad** (marnymarie@yahoo.com)

To: evanmccleerybrown@yahoo.com

Date: Thursday, January 29, 2015 5:13 AM

Dear Evan,

I LOVE this BE! The hardest "job" in life, after being a good parent, is being a good friend. But it also has its obvious great rewards as well. To BE...a friend means to be there in good times and bad times. Sad times and happy times and just "times". Obviously, I cannot begin this BE without talking about your mom, my dearest friend, Julie. She once gave me a ceramic wall hanging that says," A friend is someone who dances with you in the sunlight and walks with you in the shadows." It hangs in my kitchen and I look at it nearly every day. It is my TRUTH.

A little ironic that this BE arrived when you get to see first-hand what true friendship means. After your injury and surgery, your friends came to see you and help to cheer you up and feel better. Checking up on you. Worried about you. This is what friends do. Even if you can't do your "normal" stuff with them, they want to see you, spend time with you, hang out. Just BE in your presence.

There are entire books that have been dedicated to how to BE...a friend. And entire Hallmark sections devoted solely to friendship. So I certainly don't think I can add to the wisdom that exists already. I only hope to relate to you how deeply important to your life friends have been/are/will be.

Here is my little "Ode to A Friend"

F iercely loyal

R eassuring me; providing reality-checks and rainbows

I n celebration and strife, without fail always there

E ven to provide wisdom I may not want to hear

N ear or far, distance does not change the

D epth of our bond and connection

Friends may be older, younger, related to you or not. Don't dismiss someone as being valuable to the richness of your life simply because they may not be male or your age. And lastly I hope you are able to find your best friend in the person with whom you choose to spend your life and build your own family.
Love you dearly,

Marny

Perfectly following up on how to BE...a friend is BE...courageous. It is ever so much easier to BE...courageous when you have people behind you like a friend, supporting and believing in you.

COURAGEOUS

Subject: Be...courageous

From: **Marny Jaastad** (marnymarie@yahoo.com)

To: evanmccleerybrown@yahoo.com

Date: Friday, February 6, 2015 3:43 AM

Dear Brave Evan!

Just like the Cowardly Lion in The Wizard of Oz, I will focus on how to BE...courageous over the next week or so. There a lot of things in life that are "scary" for various reasons. True physical danger being the obvious. But then there's:

*taking that romantic risk - putting your heart in front of the world for all to see

*taking a stand for something in which you believe - even if that "something" is YOU

* confronting someone about an issue you have with them

The list could and does go on. And what we need to find courage to achieve or (to) do changes as we grow.

Good old Wikipedia defines courage as:
"the ability and willingness to confront fear, pain, danger, uncertainty, or intimidation" yes, exactly.

Courage is an interesting trait and quality. It is one that I would argue is cultivated almost solely by experience and a life well-lived.

On the flip side, I often question MYSELF in the midst of some rant of self-talk about how I'm being "chicken" or "afraid" to do something. SOMEtimes that little voice in your head overriding the "BE...courageous" mantra is trying to protect you. How does one know when to push and when to hold? You don't. That's the beauty. My risk/reward calculator basically uses the metric of "Will this cause me great harm or potential death if I get brave and do X?" Great harm is not necessarily physical. Potential mental pain/anguish is not something to which I gravitate. And though time may heal all wounds, the wounds I am willing to accept to BE...courageous and risk, have become fewer as I age.

196

I have had a good week-plus of trying to BE...courageous. I put myself out on a limb in several different ways that I would usually shy away from and/or avoid. Mentally/socially I contacted someone who I am interested in and made myself a little vulnerable. Always scary! But it was well-received so I am proud of myself. At work, I approached some new people about training which is never something I like. It's hard to essentially ask someone to spend money on you. But again, I was rewarded for my "bravery" twice and so I am encouraged to be a little more outgoing. Lastly, in the physical realm, I never have a problem pushing myself to do MORE, to go past my limit, to excel and exceed. SO to BE...courageous for me is to trust that I can do less sometimes when my body and mind might need rest. And to find out it's ok to back off at times. This is something you have probably also come to realize with your injuries this year.

"The willingness to confront" (is) such a powerful, almost loaded, phrase. How do you determine that you are not a "chicken" yet not a fool? Where is the line? Time, your gut instinct, experiences all combine to provide the line between chicken and fool. But sometimes there just has to be a leap of faith. The thrill of a little adrenaline rush of the unknown, the untested, the ill-at-ease ache in the pit of your stomach gives you the power to BE...courageous.

I'm very proud of all of the things I have witnessed you "put yourself out there" for. Testing for schools, trying out for baseball and other teams, running races, trying the guitar, going to overnight camp for the first time. All scary. All rife with uncertainty. You have faced them all and sailed through with flying colors. May you always have that passion and drive, that *willingness* to test and to BE...courageous.

Love, Marny

We are moving along into the last few BE's in the original bag o'BE's. And I am still pleasantly surprised every time I pick the next one. And so next I shall attempt to BE...appreciative. Boy do I need this one! It's good that I will have to think about all that I take for granted - because I definitely DO - and truly be grateful. I won't go overboard. Promise!

APPRECIATIVE

From: **Marny Jaastad** (marnymarie@yahoo.com)

To: evanmccleerybrown@yahoo.com

Date: Wednesday, March 4, 2015 3:40 AM

Dear Evan

Thank you so much for letting me ramble on at you for the past 2 years! And so begins how I am to BE...appreciative. I'm so grateful that I picked this BE at this time. (get it??) I had to come right out of the gates with that one.

There are two distinct meanings for how to BE...appreciative. One to be grateful, of course. The other as in fine art or someone's taste in music. As in to recognize the value in something. For our BE, I am choosing to focus on the thankful and complimentary aspect since my journey through our BE's is about self-awareness and growth.

Over the years I have maintained a weekly practice of writing - HANDWRITING - a thank you note to one of my clients or friends for just being themselves or for something particularly nice that they had done. It's pretty easy to grow to take for granted that which is regular, usual and pedantic in our everyday lives. But those people with whom we interact daily, hourly, weekly are the very ones to whom we should show our appreciation the most.

This has been quite a rocky week for the people around me and I must say I am currently *most* appreciative for the fact that I am NOT in many of the situations that they are. However, I have been able to be a resource and a "shoulder" for them. In addition to practicing the art of how to BE...appreciative, it is quite lovely to also BE appreciated from time to time. I think that this week has re-awakened my ability to see the small gifts that we offer each other all the time. We all get bogged down in the big, weighty issues of life - even in your life, I know there are big things that weigh on you. But to BE...appreciative of the person who holds a door for you or for Mom driving to pick you up at school with a snack and some dry clothes if it's been raining is really pretty special. It's that recognition that someone went out of their way, that you mean something to them, that they *care* that creates that little "awwww" in your head. That soft, in-the-pit-of-your stomach feeling of love and gratitude.

Those days when I feel my worst, whether it be tired, sad, frustrated or just grumpy in general are the hardest to BE...appreciative. But I find that when I give myself a little kick and try to look outside of my inner angst, to someone who has done something nice or improved my day, I am able to "reset" that grumpy mood. I can really BE...appreciative of all that is truly good in my life and also specifically to that person. As the saying goes, "fake it til ya make it." If you're not feeling appreciative, it often helps to FIND a little nugget of gratitude which turns your viewpoint and day around.

You probably appreciate the most that I am now done pontificating about how to BE...appreciative. But I also hope that it gives you the opportunity to look for the little things that are special in life every day. Not every day is stellar or even average but every single day there is someone to whom you can say "thanks, you made a difference."

You make a difference in my life every day. Even if I don't see, talk to or hear about you, I THINK about you every day and it brings a smile to my face,
Thanks! and Love,
Marny

We are fast-approaching the finish line of our little bag of how to BE...a person. Our next foray will be in how to BE...organized.

Well it may not be as exciting and mentally engaging as some of our other BE's *but* it is a very important component in getting yourself through your daily grind.

ORGANIZED

Subject: Be...organized

From: **Marny Jaastad** (marnymarie@yahoo.com)

To: evanmccleerybrown@yahoo.com

Date: Saturday, March 14, 2015 5:41 AM

Dear Evan,

Here is what I plan to cover in this little essay on how to BE...organized:

* definition of organization
* importance and relevance to our (you and me) little set of "BE's"
* strategies for achieving organization
* applications and examples in daily life

Ugh I feel like I'm about to give a report in school. Do you feel like you just got dropped back into class?

SO! Now that I am *organized* I can set about an orderly exploration of just how to BE...organized. (in an organized way).

Have I lost you yet in a sea of boredom? I feel the need to make this BE a little more silly and somewhat less serious in terms of the deeper, more personal implications of some of the previous BE's. I promise to not be dry about it though. Well, mostly. This is the School of Marny not Lakeside. (Evan's school)

To BE...organized is an asset not to be overrated. It is one of those things that I view as either learned and adopted early in life or lost to the wind. Look around you at school and notice the kids who are DISorganized. I think you will see it sort of pervades their lives. Organizational skills are tough to learn later in life. Mostly because they establish the "rules" of how we proceed in our "doing" lives. Versus our "being" lives - which is what most of the other BE's have covered. But since we are human doings as well as human beings, an exploration of the ways to be a successful do-er is important.
Firstly, what exactly does it mean?

Well since you didn't ask but have no choice but to read on: Having the ability to plan and accomplish things in an orderly fashion. Simple enough. But here's the part of that definition that is key: *the ability* to do so. An ability is a *learned* attribute. This is not heritable. Which for some people is a very GOOD thing since their parents could be completely DISorganized yet could teach very good organizational skills to their children (hindsight being 20/20 and all...)

In our group of 72 "BE's" why do you think it was important to include this one? It seems to me so different from all of the others in terms of personal development and growth. But in reality, it connects so many of the other BE's that it maybe should have been the first one! (Though I still love that the first one I picked was to BE...giving and it was Christmas after all. I adore irony!) Without learning to BE...organized, it would be infinitely more difficult to: BE...professional, BE...your best, BE...on top of your game, BE...prepared (for sure!), BE...productive, BE...on time. You can see that the ability to BE...organized is actually quite a good foundation for many of the other virtues that we have explored and tried to BE for the past 2 years.

There are myriad strategies for BEing organized. My personal preferred mode is THE LIST. Making lists to keep my brain on track and to "see" what it is that I must accomplish in a day or a project or over time is my strategy for getting it done. However, I have seen lists put to use to the point that they overwhelm. People's lists have lists. And in trying to BE...organized, I have witnessed complete ineffectiveness and inefficiency in the workplace. And likely that spilled over into that person's life as well. Getting bogged down in the minutiae of lists, versus the broad spectrum, can leave you spinning like the little circle on your computer......forever churning - and appearing productive - but getting nowhere...fast. Each person has to determine for themselves what works best for their brain and their lifestyle as a strategy to BE...organized.

Maybe you do the same routine or pattern of events every morning to get you out the door on time and ready. Other effective means for getting oneself in line are: taking the first few minutes of the day to mentally envision how your day will play out; at the opposite end, taking time at the end of the day to forecast the day tomorrow and prepare anything you might forget in the morning; in this digital age, (the) most commonly seen (heard) is the voice text to oneself or setting up digital reminders of things to come. Your phone tells you/beeps at you when there is an important event or you need to attend to something.

I think it's pretty self-evident the applications and importance of learning how to BE...organized is in getting through life. Whether it's a big project at school or simply figuring out how to get in all of the weekend activities you want/need to do, *having the ability* to do so in an orderly fashion makes life oh so much easier. No doubling back on yourself or double-checking that you did something. I encourage you to practice organization, since as we have seen, it's a learned skill. I have found it really becomes just your standard operating procedure and you no longer need to consciously think "How am I going to organize this or that?"

I'll spare you the recap of how to BE...organized, as I think the point has been driven (home). I hope that school continues to be something you enjoy. I think that organization is one of the things that makes school a positive and not a dreaded nuisance. Practice makes perfect! But I think you already are: PERFECT!

Love, Marny

We are headed into our homestretch of BE's! With only four to go, next we will delve into how to BE...STILL. This might be my greatest challenge yet. And yours too I would guess. We shall see!

STILL

Dear Evan

From one end of the spectrum to the other with these last two BE's. From something that comes so naturally to me: organization to something that might as well be written in Russian: STILL. This is a challenge for people like you and me, frenetic, high-energy, highly-motivated, achievers. Some people choose to meditate or do yoga or read or practice sitting and breathing. I kind of think of it as an adult "time out." As a child, we learn that a time out is not only a punishment, but an opportunity for a do-over. Sit, ponder what you have done, have no activity and try again.

However, to BE...still often has a negative connotation. That of idleness, being unproductive, lazy even. BUT I have learned over the past three years or so - too bad it took that long - that taking time to BE...still is like recharging your cell phone battery. It is necessary if you want that phone to keep functioning. No juice, no text. No stillness for the mind and body, very limited motivation to soldier on through life, at least in a pleasant, meaningful way.

I have actually started a little ritual of late which has surprised me greatly; both in terms of me actually DOING it as well as its positive effect upon me. I have taken to "making" myself watch a movie on Saturday afternoons after I come home from work and get errands done. I typically have a very difficult time sitting still at all, let alone for about 90 minutes. And though I admit I do still get up and roam around and "do" things, I am able to sit, relax, recharge and BE...still for longer periods every week.

From popular music and the song by The Fray "Be Still" to ancient wisdom and the words of Tao Te Ching:

It is not wise to dash about.

Shortening the breath causes much stress.

Use too much energy, and

You will soon be exhausted.

That is not the Natural Way.

Whatever works against this Way

Will not last long.

It would seem that we seek to BE...still at various points in our lives. I posit that the craving for stillness comes from several places. Rejuvenation as I mentioned but also possibly the fear of moving forward in time? Of our mortality? Who knows what lies deep in our unconscious that fuels our various desires and needs.

I would offer up to you and other people under the age of 20 that incorporating the practice of how to BE...still into your life NOW will be an invaluable tool for the rest of your life. Whether it be 5, 10, 15 or 30 minutes every day, that slice of the daily pie that is reserved for nothingness, UNdoingness, human BEingness is crucial and fundamental to your success and well-being.

As I begin another day of DOing, I will remind myself that to BE...still is a great art and that it is a gift that I can give to myself daily. (And in the end others benefit as well, truthfully. They get a better "Marny" with whom to interact).

Take it for a test drive. Try by starting or ending your day somewhere quiet, alone, peaceful where you can just BE......still.

Love, Marny

Onto one of our last BE's. Number SEVENTY! The investigation of how to BE...at peace. How completely appropriate after I've learned the importance of how to BE...still!

Peace Out, Evan......HA!

AT PEACE

Subject: Be...at peace

From: **Marny Jaastad** (marnymarie@yahoo.com)

To: evanmccleerybrown@yahoo.com

Date: Wednesday, April 8, 2015 3:45 AM

Dear Evan,

I almost feel as though this BE should start with a sigh. A clearing, calming, peaceful (!) kind of sigh. NOT an "I'm so irritated" sigh. It would seem to flow nicely from having practiced how to BE...still to then achieving that elusive mental state of how to BE...at peace. Peace is actually quite a sought after item (?) state of mind (?) commodity?? in our world.

We wish each other to have a peaceful sleep or to have "peace on earth" or "peace be with you." But all these "peaces" are different from that inner peace. For a body and soul to BE...at peace is a completely other state than for two countries to achieve peace or to have a peaceful night's sleep.

My observation over the years is that there are two elements that seem to generate anger/unsettledness/LACK of peace. The first being influences from others - external interactions - and the second (pretty obvious, I guess) influences from ourselves - internal interactions.

So how then to begin to address the inner and outer interactions that seek to rob us of our ambition to BE... at peace? I hope that this list below helps you to find your own path to peace when you are struggling with turmoil. Everyone's path is different and not all strategies work for everyone. These, though, I think are fairly universal across all people.

1. Someone makes you angry or irritated. Happens nearly every day, right? More often than not it's because we cannot comprehend *WHY* they have done/said the thing that is making us steam. I used to be SUCH a hothead. I'd blow up at any small thing. And it made people pretty uncomfortable – NOT at peace! – around me. And frankly, I realized that it made ME uncomfortable and nowhere near able to BE...at peace. As I started to try to stop, think, reason out WHY someone was doing/saying something I didn't like, I realized everyone sees their world – and yours – from THEIR perspective. That's all any of us can do. I now try to see how someone might view a situation in their world – which comes complete with their own problems, wishes and ambitions – which then

led them to do/say what I am angry about. It has most definitely brought my boiling point down and I have come to understand others, but more importantly, MYSELF better.

2. You meet up with your own worst enemy – yourself. Over-achievers and Type A's are notorious for beating ourselves up for our perceived failures, faults and inadequacies. Maybe you are unhappy about a play you made in baseball or you didn't like the comments a teacher made on an assignment. I was a habitual "ruer" – as in I rued things that I had done or had occurred in the past. I desperately wanted to "go back" to that time; to rectify the wrong that I felt I had done. I just wanted to "fix" things. Well the truth is, things are broken. We cannot always do/act/be the person in our minds who is the ideal, the pinnacle of perfection. The constant perseverating over the past, over what is uncontrollable left me most definitely in a mental state far from peaceful.

Though it is still a challenge, one of the greatest tactics I have learned is how to use those moments I regret as learning aids. Yes, learning is lifelong. I tell myself to look to the future and how, going forward, I will manage a situation like that if I find myself there again. The past is never to be forgotten but we should use it as a tool to forge a better future.

3. Forgive. You do not have to forget, as the saying says, but forgiveness is monumental. Both with yourself and with others – especially your brothers and parents – being able to forgive transgressions will foster peace in your life and theirs. Tougher than it may seem, truly learning to forgive takes some pretty deep reflection and self-awareness. My own struggles with learning to "let go" of a gripe have been challenging. I have often had those little fantasies of wanting to get even with or seek revenge upon someone. How peaceful can that be? NOT! My mind would stew and percolate over the event or hurtful words I felt. I finally realized that this got me nowhere and also got in the way of enjoying the current life I was living. I try to remind myself when I am angry with someone, or with myself, that my energy - physical and emotional - should be devoted to ME. To the things I WANT to do and feel. My energy should not be "stolen" from me. Gaining the ability to forgive actually sets you free more than the other person.

To BE...at peace is such an elusive place to find. You cannot GoogleMaps it or ask Siri how to get there. It is an internal exploration and each person's path will be different. I wish for you that you are able to start down your path earlier in life than I was able to. Notice your reactions to the world and to yourself. Make no judgments upon them. Use them to further your understanding of life and its challenges. Teach yourself to take actions and use words that will help you in your ability to BE...at peace.

Pretty heavy stuff at times, I know. As we move along to our last two BE's, I am getting a little excited and a little melancholy at the thought of the end of this little road in our lives. These explorations have definitely aided me in moving toward a person who is able to BE...at peace.

 Love, Marny

Our second to last investigation will be to learn to BE...true blue. Huh. OK.....this is going to be another of those head-scratcher ones. Lots of meanings to this. I know that I am forever true blue to YOU, Dear Evan.

Have a great day and take a little time to reflect on how to BE...at peace every day.

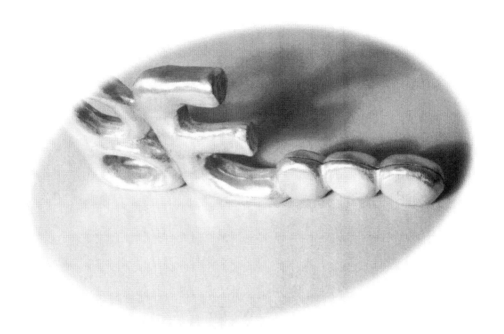

TRUE BLUE

From: **Marny Jaastad** (marnymarie@yahoo.com)

To: evanmccleerybrown@yahoo.com

Date: Saturday, April 25, 2015 5:37 AM

Dear Ever-loyal Evan:

I am ever so true blue to YOU!

HUH.....this one is definitely going to take some interesting twists and turns I think. I wasn't sure where I might head with this when I first picked it but I know that it does describe the way I feel about you and your family. It's a more broad-reaching BE than most of our others. It's not about being in a specific moment or achieving a particular state of being. In essence it really is simply ABOUT BEing... That said, how might I convey to you and myself the importance of being that true blue person?

Of course I start with good old Wiki. "The origin of the phrase 'true blue' is supposed to derive from the blue cloth that was made at Coventry, England in the late Middle Ages. The town's dyers had a reputation for producing material that didn't fade with washing, that is, it remained 'fast' or 'true'." Something you could always count on." I'd like to think that to my dearest friends and family, I am something they can always count on. And PLAN to count on. More than simply stating that "I am always there for you," your actions demonstrate that fact and provide comfort and security in the knowledge that you ARE there, that your support will not fade over time.

Though I pride myself on the ability to always BE...true blue, I find I have spent more time this week "checking in" on my special people. Especially your mom as she nears the completion of her PhD. A little note, mental "fist bump" or cheer-leading from afar can turn a bad day around or make a good day into a great one.

The thing about BEing...TRULY true blue is that it is *genuine*. By genuine I mean that there is nothing contrived, selfish or forced about your actions or your intent. Sometimes when we do things for others it is to gain a benefit for ourselves as well. To BE...true blue you must release all attachments to "pay backs" or "only if's." Your "people" never owe you anything for your loyalty and even when (*especially* when) they seem ungrateful, unhappy, grumpy and

213

generally no fun to be around you pour on that moral support and stand-by-you-ness.

There are some other places that we might look to how to emulate how to BE... true blue. Dogs are the perfect example. Look at Tucker. He is as loyal to you as they come. Anyone can simply utter, "Tucker, Evan needs you!" and what happens? WHAM! Instant dog in your bed. No expectation of a reward, other than your love and affection. Just a dog and his boy. Bound together by this invisible thread of trueness. It would be a stretch to say the sun is true blue, but you get the idea. Do you ever consider that you might get up one day and there would be NO sun? No. Well at least I don't short of watching Armageddon-themed sci-fi movies. And I hope that you never wake up to consider that one day I might not be there. Because if there is one thing I can assure you of for the rest of my time on this earth, I will BE the TRUEST of BLUE for YOU!

A little sappy and a little out there with the sun reference, I know. It is honestly how deeply important I feel this next-to-last BE is in all of our lives. Think about Haden and your other friends. These are your true blues. That would be a good name for a clubhouse and its members – The True Blues. Ok ok. Enough. I think I am seriously procrastinating pulling that last little notecard out of the burlap bag it came in to reveal our final search into the Land of Be...

And with that I will tell you one last time that I truly and blue-ly love you. To the ends of the earth, to the moon and back and through every black hole that exists (I think that's an oxymoron).

Love you,

Marny

Here we go.....(there's a drumroll in my head right now) for the final BE in our exploration. And that would (be) BE...**BOLD**!!! And we're off to the races on that one.

BOLD

From: **Marny Jaastad** (marnymarie@yahoo.com)

To: evanmccleerybrown@yahoo.com

Date: Tuesday, May 5, 2015 4:48 AM

DEAR EVAN!! (How's that for BOLD??)

The very first thing that came to my mind upon pulling this short, succinct, powerful last BE from its bag was this is easy! Just BE...YOURSELF! And by that I mean do not ever have fear of showing who you are, standing up for your convictions and beliefs, BEing BOLD in the face of adversity or even mild discomfort. (Haha)

And BOLD have I been so far this week. It's amazing what effect even the smallest suggestion inserted into your subconscious can have on your actions. I found myself taking actions and making decisions about my life this past week that were truly bold in nature. I had a "win" at work with an issue that needed to be corrected in my paycheck and I made a personal decision about my commitment to my work versus to myself that has been hugely liberating. Maybe I ought to try this BE...BOLD stuff more often!

Though I know that being considered BOLD can also have a negative connotation at times, the positive far outweighs the allusion to ego, haughtiness or aggression. So what are the actions we can take in life that will encourage our BOLD behavior? Obviously this can be defined by each person differently depending upon what our life challenges might be or upon the specific circumstances in which we find ourselves needing to BE...BOLD.

One tactic that I find useful for helping me to BE...BOLD is to think of someone who I admire for their courage and try to emulate them. I envision this person in my current situation and ask...."What would so-and-so do in my shoes?" And then I decide if this is the right action for me to take or how else I might bring out my boldness utilizing that person's power and strength.

Hesitation is a boldness-killer. For myself, to truly BE...BOLD requires no stopping to think about my actions too much. Sometimes the most unexpected (either by you or by others!) things are the ones that get you the furthest. While I would certainly not be an advocate of acting rashly, there are times when too much rumination leads to stagnancy and being "stuck" in a spin cycle like your washing machine.

Lastly I would offer that with as much strength as it takes to say YES it takes even more to say NO! If you are made to feel uncomfortable or uneasy about a situation - whether that be peer pressure, a request from a coach or other adult, or just your own actions which may create a question mark in your mind - find the courage and BE...BOLD. Just say NO if you KNOW it is the wrong thing for you.

The tricky side of BEing...BOLD is that as a younger person, it is often perceived as disrespectful or out of line when directed at an older person. To finesse your ability to get your point across and to be heard, it is important to be both direct, reasoned and calm. One of my 14 year old clients is on the track team at school and has gotten injured a couple of times as the coach has wanted her to be in and train for longer events. She is more interested in doing sprint distance events and working on her speed. We discussed whether it would be better for her parents to talk with the coach or for her to advocate for herself. She took on the challenge! I was very proud of her and it was a good lesson for her to learn. She crafted her arguments well, made a specific appointment to talk with the coach and kept herself from being emotional. She was respectful to him as her coach and as an adult but made it clear that her needs (and her health!) were just as important as his goals for the team. They reached a compromise and everyone is pleased. Even better, the coach definitely has a better attitude toward her. A great result of her decision to BE...BOLD.

As the German writer Goethe said, "Boldness has genius, power and magic in it."

As we come to the end of our exploration of how to BE...in life, Evan, remember always that I do find you to be all of the above: a genius, powerful and magical! In all that you pursue and become in life, always keep that nugget in the back of your mind and BE...BOLD and true to yourself.

With great love and gratitude for all that you have taught me and helped me to think about over these past two years and four months,

Marny

The deepest of thanks and gratitude

There are so many people who have been fundamental to the creation of this little nugget of wisdom(s). There were unsuspecting clients who helped me recognize and examine these attributes in the real world. Julie McCleery Brown: friend, mother of Evan, sister-from-another-mister, co-competitor and lover of words and thought. My parents, Sig Jaastad and Judy Jaastad, who always encourage and support my endeavors – be they creative or physical, foolish or prudent - and lead by example with their own. Laura Asamen who did me the honor of reading through all of the BE's without knowing who Evan really was but just because she wanted to help me. And to The Sage of Self-publishing, Stu Schreiber, thank you for letting me pick your brain, follow you around the gym asking you questions and for helping me to navigate my creative path.

And of course, EVAN himself. The now almost-15 year-old godson who is the heart of this book and my life. I cannot begin to offer my thanks for reading my words and for, I hope, understanding their meaning. May he find some application of them to his life now and in the future.

Made in the USA
Middletown, DE
22 December 2016